Microsoft Word Problem Solver

Lester C. Karplus

Scott, Foresman and Company
Glenview, Illinois   London

Library of Congress Cataloging-in-Publication Data

Karplus, Lester C.
    Microsoft Word problem solver / Lester C. Karplus
    p. cm. -- (Problem solver series)
    ISBN 0-673-46147-5
    1. Microsoft Word (Computer program) 2. Word
processing. I. Title. II Series.
Z52.5.M52K36   1989
652.5536--dc20   89-10787
                                      CIP

        1 2 3 4 5 6 EBI 94 93 92 91 90 89

ISBN 0-673-46147-5

Notice of Liability

The information in this book is distributed on an "As Is" basis, without warranty. Neither the author nor Scott, Foresman and Company shall have any liability to customer or any other person or entity with respect to any liability, loss, or damage caused or alleged to be caused directly or indirectly by the programs contained herein. This includes, but is not limited to, interruption of service, loss of data, loss of business or anticipatory profits, or consequential damages from the use of the programs.

Scott, Foresman professional books are available for bulk sales at quantity discounts. For information, please contact Marketing Manager, Professional Books Group, Scott, Foresman and Company, 1900 East Lake Avenue, Glenview, IL 60025.

Foreword
by Ralph Blodgett

The **Problem Solver** book in your hands represents a new concept in computer book publishing. Rather than listing features of a program one after another, this series of books offers—in a quickly accessible format—answers to typical problems that users encounter when using a particular piece of software.

We designed the series as reference guides that you will want to keep next to your computer for quick inspection. Inside you will find brief, concise answers to 100—150 real-life problems that thousands of others before you have encountered. All of the answers are found on one, or at most two, pages.

When you encounter a problem, use this book to quickly find a solution. Let it be your resource guide to get you out of sticky situations that other books fail to warn about. In fact, if you are a beginner or intermediate user, this book will fill an important gap left by your manual and other books on the market.

Other books in the **Problem Solver** series include:
- **dBase IV Problem Solver**
- **DOS 4.0 Problem Solver**
- **Microsoft Excel Problem Solver**
- **PageMaker Problem Solver**
- **Sprint Problem Solver**
- **Ventura Problem Solver**
- **WordPerfect Problem Solver**

Table of Contents

How to Use This Book   viii
Chapter 1   Beginning WORD   1
Chapter 2   Dictionary   13
Chapter 3   Editing   23
Chapter 4   Files   43
Chapter 5   Format   55
Chapter 6   Graphics   81
Chapter 7   Macros and Glossaries   93
Chapter 8   Merging   103
Chapter 9   Outline   113
Chapter 10   Printer   119
Chapter 11   Style Sheets   137
Chapter 12   Tables and Indexes   147
Chapter 13   Windows   155
Index   161

How to Use This Book

Introduction

The Microsoft WORD 5.0 Problem Solver provides the user a unique approach to higher word processing productivity. While Microsoft provides the user an excellent manual, the Problem Solver focuses on the common problems experienced by users of Microsoft WORD.

This book was compiled from thousands of questions users have had about WORD. These questions were obtained from technical support at Microsoft, the Compuserve WORD forum and the author's experience in teaching and supporting Microsoft WORD.

Organization

The Microsoft WORD 5.0 Problem Solver is organized into thirteen topics ranging from common activities such as editing and printing to the more unique features of WORD such as outlining, tables and indexing. The first section, Beginning WORD, includes many of the problems a new user might encounter getting started with WORD. The thirteen sections are arranged in alphabetical order.

Within each section, one or two pages are dedicated to one specific problem and solution. The problem generally is posed in the form of a question. The solution is provided as a procedure or narrative response.

The problem/solution is further summarized using a phrase or key word that emphasizes the feature of WORD being discussed in the solution. These key words or phrases are placed as headers at the top of the page. Within each section, these phrases are arranged in alphabetical order.

Finding Solutions

This book may be used several ways to find solutions. First, check the Table of Contents for the appropriate section. Then scan the section headers for key words that might provide the answer.

Because many sections have interrelated topics, reviewing several questions and answers within a section may provide a better answer to your problem. A general reading of the entire section also may be useful.

Many problems cross over into other topics. By using the extensive index provided in the Microsoft WORD 5.0 Problem Solver, you will obtain all of the references to a specific topic.

Syntax

This book has been prepared for the beginning and intermediate user. Most solutions, therefore, have been oriented to using the WORD menu commands. While many solutions have a "quick key" alternative, they generally have been left out to avoid potential confusion for the new user.

The Esc key has been left out of the manuscript intentionally as it is similarly left out of the Microsoft Manual. To execute any WORD menu command you must first press Esc.

To execute a menu command, the instructions in this book use the same words that appear in the menu. To execute the command, you type the first letter of the command or, in some cases, the capitalized letter in the command word. For example, the operational instruction to "Select the Print Merge Print command" would be implemented by typing, Esc PMP and pressing Enter. The instruction to "Select the Format pOsition command" would be implemented by typing Esc PO and pressing Enter.

When options are available within a menu command, they are referred to as fields and the field name is enclosed in quotation marks. For example, an instruction might read: "In the Options menu, the field "show borders" may be turned on by selecting Yes."

Whenever more than one key is simultaneously required to execute a command, it is indicated with a + sign. Alt + F8 means you must hold down the Alt key and then press F8. If a style sheet is attached, the speed formatting keys require that an X be added before pressing the appropriate format key. Alt + XB, for example, is the command to bold text if a style sheet is attached.

You will find the structure to the many solutions in this book concise and easy to follow. For further explanations, consult your WORD manuals.

Chapter 1

Beginning WORD

Beginning WORD, Automatic Execution

How can I start WORD from my hard disk without all the steps of changing directories?

To execute WORD without changing directories every time you begin and end a session, you must either incorporate a menu system on your hard disk or create a batch file to change the directories for you. To create a batch file that executes WORD by typing the command WP, you must first be in the root directory and then create a DOS batch file. To do this:

1. Type CD \ to be sure you are in the root directory.
2. Type COPY CON WP.BAT to instruct the computer to create a batch file.
3. Type CD \WORD5 and press Enter.

4. Type WORD and press Enter.
5. Type CD \ and press Enter.
6. Press F6 and press Enter.

If you wish to execute WORD automatically whenever you boot your computer, substitute AUTOEXEC.BAT for WP.BAT in the above instructions. Be sure you don't already have an AUTOEXEC.BAT file before doing this. If you do have one, you may modify it by:

1. Type EDLIN AUTOEXEC.BAT.
2. Type L to list the contents.
3. Type I to insert new lines.
4. Type the instructions in lines 3-5 above.
5. Press Control + C.
6. Type E and press Enter to end the session.

How can I load a file automatically when I execute WORD?

If you know with which document you are going to start a WORD session, you may load it as you execute WORD. Type WORD and the document name and the document is automatically displayed when WORD is executed. For example, to load the document LETTER, type WORD LETTER.

If you are using a menu system with your computer and regularly require the same document to be loaded when you start WORD, you may add an autoexec macro to load the file. The Autoexec macro, a feature of WORD, must be created and stored in the file called NORMAL.GLY.

To create an autoexec macro to load a file called LETTER, at any time in the edit mode of WORD:

1. Press Shift + F3 to turn on the Record Macro command.

2. Select Transfer Load and type LETTER. Press Enter.

3. Press Shift + F3 to turn off the Record Macro command.

4. Type autoexec for the macro name. Or you may add the ^ and press Control + A to have the ability to execute this macro from within WORD.

What does it mean when a dotted line appears on the screen while I am typing?

A dotted line appearing while you are typing indicates that the automatic page break feature is turned on. Based on the margins you have created in the Format Division Margins command, the number of lines on a page is counted automatically. The dotted line indicates each time you have reached the page's bottom.

Turning off this feature will prevent automatic repagination in your document if you make a format change that affects every page. Especially in long documents, there can be a long wait time. If you want to turn off this feature, select the Options command and choose Manual in the "paginate" field. Your document will still paginate automatically when it is printed.

You may enter page breaks manually at any time by pressing Control + Shift + Enter. You also may change the page break locations by selecting the Print Repaginate command. Select Yes to control the location of the page break. WORD displays each page break. You may move the page break or remove any existing manual page break when prompted with the option to remove them..

To distinguish between manual and automatic page breaks, WORD places the dots together in a manual break and alternates a space in the automatic break.

I've seen other people in the office with slower cursor movement than I have. How can I slow mine down?

Cursor speed may be adjusted in the Options menu in the field "cursor speed." The default value is 3 and the speed range is from 0, slow, to 9, fast.

If you select too fast a speed, you may overrun your target location and too slow a speed may be somewhat frustrating. Play around with the speed until you are comfortable.

You may notice a decrease in cursor speed in Graphics mode. If you move back and forth from the Graphics display mode to the text display mode, you may wish to change your cursor speed.

I would like to optimize the amount of text displayed on the screen, eliminate the menu and borders and change the colors so that they are easier to read. What steps should I take to do this?

Display characteristics are controlled in the Options menu. To optimize your screen display area, here are the options available:

1. The "show menu" field selects whether or not the menu is to be displayed at the bottom of the screen. If you choose No, text is displayed in the menu location until the Esc key is pressed. Whenever the Esc key is pressed, the menu is alternately displayed and removed.

2. The border takes up an extra character and two lines on the screen. The "show border" field controls the display of it. If you turn it off, some of the mouse functions are disabled, such as splitting windows horizontally .

3. There are a number of options in the "display mode" field, depending on the type of monitor you are using. You most likely can display 43 lines of text on the screen in either text or graphics mode. Press F1 to see the options available. You may switch back and forth between a graphics and text selection using Alt + F9. WORD remembers the last two selections.

4. Color choices makes screen reading easier. Because everyone has their own preference, the "color" field is used to select

6

various colors for backgrounds, borders, messages, and character attributes. Press F1 to view the selections. Use PgUp and PgDn or point with the mouse to change the selections.

Why can't I move my cursor past the diamond?

The diamond is the symbol WORD uses for the end of the document. Because it is the end, you cannot go beyond it. If you are trying to enter more space, press the Enter key and the end mark will be moved forward.

When you first execute WORD or begin a new document, a line is automatically inserted at the beginning of the document. This is a change from 4.0 which started the document with the end mark. This extra line allows the entry of new formatting at the beginning of the document as the end mark cannot be formatted.

When you format a division, you will notice that the end mark also follows the division mark. (The division mark is a double dotted line that indicates the end of a specific group of page formats.) The end mark cannot be deleted or edited.

I am used to setting tabs on my typewriter that correspond to the number of characters typed. In WORD, the number of characters seems to be different. How can I change this?

The default setting in WORD for Tabs is based on inches and the default value is one-half inch. To change the method of measurement, select the Option command and choose either P10 or P12 in the "measurement" field. The selection depends on whether you are using a 10 or 12 pitch type style. A 10 pitch type style has 10 characters per inch and a 12 pitch has 12 characters per inch.

You will notice the next time you select the Option command the "default tab width" changes to the number of characters. For example, if you did not change the "default tab width" field, the entry now displays "5 p10."

It is recommended that you use this type of tab setting only for fixed space, (not proportionally spaced) type styles.

The mouse on my computer makes Word slower than computers that friends of mine use. Can I turn the mouse off periodically?

It is being in graphics mode that slows down the display. To speed up the display, switch to a text mode.

To switch to a text mode, select the Options command and change the "display" field to a text mode. (Press F1 to see the display mode options.) The mouse is still enabled but displays as a box instead of a pointer. If you aren't going to be using the mouse, move the box to a corner of the screen so it is less distracting.

To completely disable the mouse, you must turn it off outside WORD, however if you remain in graphics mode you will not see any major change in speed by turning it off. Check your mouse software instruction manual for information on disabling the mouse.

When I change the font in my document to a smaller size, part of the document runs off the right side of the screen. How can I see the entire document without having to scroll the window to the right side?

When text runs off of the screen, you are in the layout mode. To change to the display mode, select the Options command and choose the No option in the "show layout" field.

The "show layout" option provides the user with the ability to see the way the document will print. The line on the display corresponds directly to the line on the printer. This option should not be confused with the Print preView option which shows the document printout graphically on the screen.

The layout mode is indicated on the status line, located at the bottom of the display, with the initials LY.

What is the meaning and function of the Transfer command?

The new user is often confused by the concept and terminology of the Transfer command. Once this command is understood, WORD makes much more sense.

The Transfer command contains all of the selections needed to move documents back and forth from the screen to the disk. They are in effect "transferred" back and forth. Loading a file consists of transferring it from the disk to the screen and saving a file consists of transferring it back to the disk.

The Transfer command provides the options to load, merge, and save files, load, merge, and save glossaries, change the default directory, rename or delete files, and clear the screen.

When working with several open Windows, the Transfer AllSave command saves every document so you don't have to individually save them before closing all the windows.

Chapter 2

Dictionary

Our office frequently produces technical reports and manuals that require technical words not found in the dictionary. How do we avoid these being shown as misspellings?

There are three alternatives to add words to WORD's dictionary system. They may be added to the main dictionary, a special user dictionary, or to a document dictionary that is unique to the document being checked.

The appropriate selection in this case would be to create a user dictionary. This keeps spell-checking more efficient when searches for these technical words is not required. The user dictionary acts as an optional supplement to the main dictionary.

To create a new user dictionary and add words:

1.   Type a list of the words you wish to have in your new user dictionary in a new document. Place one word on each line.

2.   Sort the words into alphabetical order using the Library Autosort command.

3.   Save this file using the Transfer Save command. Type the filename, then a period, and the letters .CMP as a file extension to identify it as a user dictionary. For example if you wish to call the dictionary TECH, type TECH.CMP. Select the "Text-only" option by pressing the down arrow key and typing "T." Be sure to save it in the same directory as the main dictionary.

To use this dictionary when checking a document:

1.   Select Library Spell or press Alt + F6.

2.   When the first unknown word is reached, select Options.

3.   Type the name of your dictionary. This user dictionary will remain present until you select another one.

When I produce large documents in a spreadsheet, I would like to use the WORD spell checker. Is this possible?

WORD can spell check only a document that is first loaded as a WORD document. To check your spreadsheet file, you must first print it to a file.

To load the file, you must specify the complete path and filename used to write the spreadsheet file. For example, if you saved the file as OUTPUT.PRN in the directory \LOTUS, you must execute Transfer Load and type C:\LOTUS\OUTPUT.PRN to load the file. The spelling may be checked then by executing the Library Spell command.

Because the import of an ASCII file from WORD to the spreadsheet may be more trouble than it's worth, it is a good idea to mark all the spelling errors in the document. This is done by selecting the revision marks feature of WORD. Then print the document and manually correct the errors displayed in the ASCII printed version of the spreadsheet.

To display the revision marks, select Format revision-Marks, Options. Select yes to "add revision marks." If you want further indication of an error, you may also mark changes with the revision side bar character within the same menu option.

To check the spelling:

1. Select Library Spell or press Alt + F6.
2. Complete the spelling check.
3. Print the document to see the revision marks to make changes to the original document.

We often have to send correspondence to other countries in which their language is used. Can I use a foreign language dictionary with WORD?

Because of the ability to create a user dictionary, you may import any dictionary that is available in an ASCII file and is in alphabetical order. Follow these steps:

1. Be sure the target dictionary is in an ASCII format. This means it can be read with the DOS TYPE command and that the file has no non-text characters.
2. Load the file, using the entire file name, with the Transfer Load command.
3. Save the file with the extension .CMP. You now have a foreign language dictionary. It is defined as a user dictionary and may be loaded, using the Options selection, whenever the Library Spell command is selected.

Note: Check with Microsoft for the availability of third party dictionaries.

I have been working with the spell-checker frequently and it has worked fine. Now all of a sudden I can't get it to work.

The path name may have been inadvertently changed in the Options menu. Look for the file SPELL-AM.LEX. It is most likely in the \WORD5 directory. However, if it was installed in another directory, select the appropriate directory.

Select the Options menu and enter the correct path name on the speller path option. For example, type C:\WORD5\SPELL-AM.LEX

User defined dictionaries must be specified on the Library Spell menu. Select Options and type the full path and file name of the dictionary required.

When completing an edit, I often find it unnecessary to check the entire document for spelling errors. Can I check just one word or a part of the document?

WORD can check selective parts of the document. It begins the spell check process at the cursor location and continues to the end of the document. When the check is completed to the end of the document, the user is prompted with the choice to continue checking from the beginning of the document or quit the process.

If you wish to check only a word or a few paragraphs to save time, simply highlight the words to be checked. Place the cursor at the starting point to check, press F6, and move the cursor to the end of the selection to check. Then, execute the Library Spell command.

Note: Remember, if a spell check occurs more quickly than expected, it may be the result of a highlighted portion of the document.

Our office frequently sends letters to new clients. The client's names, however, show as misspellings. How do we avoid these as misspellings without making the dictionary too large?

There are two options for handling proper names without them making the Standard dictionary too large. Enter names into either a User-defined dictionary or a Document dictionary.

If you will address the person frequently in the course of business, it is advisable to use the User-defined option. If you only need to refer to the current letter, add the name to the Document dictionary.

To add the name to a Document dictionary, select the Add option in Library Spell when the name appears as incorrect. Then choose the Document option.

The process is similar when adding the name to a User-defined dictionary except you must check to see the correct dictionary has been selected. Choose Options first and type the name of the dictionary. (If it is a new dictionary, type the file name and the dictionary is created.) Once the correct dictionary is selected, choose the Add option from the Library Spell menu. Finally choose User-defined to have the name added to the dictionary.

I have certain pet words that I frequently misspell. Is there a way to have WORD automatically correct these errors?

When a commonly misspelled word is displayed, you may have WORD remember it, and automatically correct it whenever it is encountered in the Library Spell routine. Use the following procedure:

1. Select Library Spell.
2. When the word you wish to have automatically corrected is displayed, proceed to correct as you would normally.
3. Before you press Enter, select the Remember option by pressing the Tab key. Type Y for Yes to complete the entry.

This entry will be saved for future WORD sessions.

How can I look up the meaning of a word with WORD?

You cannot use the dictionary features of WORD in a traditional sense. To look up a meaning of a word, you need to use the Thesaurus. This will give you synonyms of the word. You can then replace the word you are looking up with one of the synonyms if you wish. To look up a word:

1. Be sure the cursor is positioned anywhere in the word you wish to look up.
2. Select the Library thEsuarus command.
3. The synonyms are displayed.
4. If you wish to look further, select one of the words in the list and press Control + 6.

To enter a choice in your document:

1. Move the cursor to the word you wish to use.
2. Press Enter. The word is automatically substituted in the document.

To leave the Thesaurus without making a change, press Esc.

Note: You also may wish to buy an add on dictionary that is accessed using the Library Run command.

Chapter 3

Editing

Edit, Backspace Not Working

The Backspace key intermittently does not work and all I get is a beep. What causes this?

The Backspace key does not function when WORD is in Overtype mode and the cursor has not been moved to the right. You can tell if WORD is in Overtype mode by checking for the OT initials at the bottom right hand corner of the screen.

If the cursor has been moved to the right when in Overtype mode, the Backspace key will function until the cursor reaches the character at which the Overtype mode was selected.

To turn off Overtype, press F5. The OT initials disappear from the bottom of the screen. The Backspace key is made fully functional.

The F5 key is a toggle that alternately switches on and off the Overtype mode every time it is pressed. When not in Overtype mode, it is in Insert mode. Characters are inserted directly to the left of the cursor location.

It seems that I frequently leave the Caps Lock on, resulting in the reversing of the desired upper and lower case. Is there a quick way to reverse this error?

In WORD 4.0, changing cases with Format Character allowed the user to change to all upper case only. An additional feature in 5.0 allows the user three options to change character case.

First, highlight the words you wish to change case. Then press Control + F4 to toggle through the three options for changing case. The first option is all upper case, the second is first letter only upper case, and the third is all lower case.

For example, if you typed the following:

jOHN jONES

Highlight the text and,
Press Control + F4,   JOHN JONES
Press Control + F4 again,   John Jones
Press Control + F4 again,   john jones

When creating a table, it sometimes is necessary to delete a column of data and move it to another location. Is there a way to do this without deleting and inserting data one line at a time?

Moving a column that has been created with a Tab is as easy as moving any other text, with one additional command:

1. First you must be able to see all of the non-printing symbols. If you cannot see them, select the Options command from the main menu and change the setting "show non-printing symbols" to "All."

2. Next, move the cursor to the upper left hand corner of the column that you wish to move.

3. Press Shift + F6 to turn on the column selection.

4. Highlight the entire column by pressing the arrow. You must include the trailing Tab characters, (the one that follows the column).

5. Press Delete to place the column in the "scrap." The scrap is shown on the bottom line and holds the last deletion made.

6. Move the cursor to the character which will begin the new column.

7. Press Insert to reenter the text in the new location.

(If you are moving the last column, you must add Tab characters to the end of each row before moving it.)

When I save or load a file with a long path description and incorrectly type it, it can be quite cumbersome to retype it. Can WORD edit the command field entry instead of requiring it to be retyped?

If you wish to change an entry, the first keystroke typed clears the line and starts a new entry. To edit the entry instead of clearing it, use the F9 and F10 keys.

The F9 key moves the cursor to the left in the field and F10 moves it to the right. The backspace and delete keys both function to remove characters. The Overtype mode however is not carried into this function and entries are made only in insert mode.

I want to create special graphic characters using the extended character set. How do I get these characters to display on the screen?

Special graphics characters to create everything from boxes to shading are available in what is referred to as the extended character set. A chart of these characters is available in Appendix A of the Reference to Microsoft Word manual.

To have these characters display on your monitor, hold down the Alt key and type the number of the character on the number pad. For example the character code for the infinity sign, "∞" is 236. To select this code, hold down the Alt key and type 236.

Displaying the codes is fairly easy. Getting them to print is another story. Some printers do not support the printing of the Extended Character Set.

WORD provides a macro to test your printer's capability. It is called "character_test.mac" and is available in the MACRO.GLY glossary file. To load the file, select Transfer Glossary Load, and type the path in which it is located and then the file name, MACRO.GLY. To execute it, select the Insert command, press F1 to see the options, choose character_test.mac and press Enter. A sample of all the available type faces is printed.

When preparing sales and marketing reports, our office often needs to indicate the source of information in the document, but it should not be printed. How can this be done?

WORD provides the user with the ability to create hidden text. The Hidden text feature may be optionally displayed on the screen and printed. Hidden text allows you to create within the document notes that are not printed. Hidden text is formatted similarly to bolding or underlining. The user may choose then to optionally display or not display the hidden text. Hidden text also may be optionally printed or not printed.

Hidden text is formatted by first highlighting the text. Press F6 and move the cursor keys to highlight the text. Then select Yes in the "hidden" field of the Format Character option or press Alt + E.

To display or hide text on screen that is formatted as hidden text, select the Yes or No options from the "show hidden text" field of the Options menu.

To print hidden text with the document, select Yes in the "hidden text" field of the Print Options menu.

I often find it cumbersome to extend the cursor when highlighting large amounts of text. Is there a more efficient way to do this?

When the F6 key is pressed, the highlight may be extended in a number of different ways. Here are some of the keys you can use to extend the highlight.

F7/F8	Prior/Next word
Shift+F7/F8	Prior/Next sentence
F9/F10	Prior/Next paragraph
PgUp/PgDn	Prior/Next screen
Ctrl+PgUp/PgDn	Start/End document
Home/End	Start/End line
Ctrl+Home/End	Start/End display
Esc Jump	Move to any page

The cursor also may be extended to highlight text by holding down the Shift key and pressing any of the Arrow keys. This is particularly useful when you have text not defined by any of the above parameters.

If you have a mouse, highlighting text is as easy as pointing to the starting character, pressing the left button, moving to the last character to be highlighted, and releasing the left button.

Is there an advantage to using a mouse to edit?

This is generally a matter of personal preference. Some people find it easier to move around the screen by moving a mouse, while others feel they have more control by pressing keys.

With a mouse you are not confined to moving straight up and down or side to side. Instead, you can move it diagonally across the screen, placing the cursor quickly where you wish to edit.

The use of a mouse is a more visual activity and as a result there is less keystroke decision making. For example, to open a window with a mouse, you move the arrow on the right side bar where you want the window to start and press the right mouse button. On the keyboard, this takes at least 5 keystrokes.

Using the mouse, on the other hand, in the graphics mode slows down your computer. On an XT type machine, this slow speed may be unacceptable.

Our office prepares memos that often repeat information from previous documents. Is there a way to avoid retyping this information?

There are two ways to retrieve information from another document. If it is a short memo, the fastest way to retrieve the information is to merge the two documents together and then delete the unwanted information. (The two files remain intact).

To merge two documents, load the first document, then select Transfer Merge and enter the file name of the second document. The second document is merged into the first at the location of the first.

If you want to retrieve just a paragraph or so out of another document, it is better to create a window, load the document and copy the desired portion to the new document. To copy text using windows:

1. Open a new window by selecting Windows, Split, Horizontal, 10 to split the window at line 10. Press Tab and select Y to clear the new window.

2. Select Transfer Load and load the document from which you will transfer information.

3. Highlight each section you wish to transfer.

4. Select the Copy command. Press Enter to copy it to the scrap.

5. Press F1 to switch to the original window.

6. Locate the cursor where you wish to place the copied text. Press Insert. The text in the scrap is added to the new document.

7. To close the window, select the Window Close command and type 2 to enter the window number.

While editing a paragraph, the format suddenly changed. What caused this and how can I correct it?

The paragraph can change its format in the edit mode due to the paragraph marker being deleted. Because the format for a paragraph is controlled by the paragraph marker, inadvertent deletion will cause the paragraph to merge with the paragraph that follows it. Both paragraphs adopt the format of the second paragraph.

If you discover the error right after you make it, select the Undo command to return the paragraph to its original condition. If you have continued to edit and then discover the error, you must reformat the paragraph with the Format Paragraph command.

Note: To see the paragraph markers, select the Option command and select Partial in the "show non-printing symbols" field.

Edit, Search and Replace not working

Sometimes, when I do a search, or a replace, no selections are found even though I can see one right on the screen. Why does this happen only occasionally?

There are a couple of reasons why a Search or Replace command does not work.

First, be sure you have not highlighted extra characters. If more than one character is highlighted, Search and Replace commands search only the highlighted area. (This of course is useful for doing specialized searches.)

The second reason you may not find text is because the cursor is below the text being searched. This is resolved by either moving the cursor to the beginning of the document (Control + PgUp) or by setting the direction in the Search or Replace command to search "Up."

Although not as common, it is also possible that the case sensitivity is set to Yes. If it is, then only the exact match of upper or lower case letters is searched. This is changed in the Search or Replace commands.

I would like to replace all of the underlined text with italic text. Is there a way to do this automatically?

Searching for formats uses a similar procedure to searching for text. Place the cursor before the first selection to be searched and select Format sEarch. You are then prompted to select either a character or paragraph search. Select the format type, such as bold, italic, or underline, you wish to find. Press Shift + F4 to continue the search.

To do a Search and Replace to replace underlined text with italic text:

1. Move the cursor to any point before the first text to be changed.
2. Select the Format repLace command.
3. Select Character from the menu.
4. Select Yes or No to have WORD confirm each replacement. No makes an automatic replacement of the selection.
5. Move the cursor to select the underline format and type Y. This is the format to be replaced. Press Enter when the selection is complete.
6. The replacement selections are displayed. Repeat the same procedure in step 5, selecting the italic feature. Press Enter.

If you selected Yes to the Confirm prompt, WORD will stop at every occurrence to confirm the replacement. If you selected No, WORD will automatically make every replacement and return you to the original location of the cursor.

Note: The capital E in sEarch and the capital L in repLace are used to indicate the actual letter pressed to execute the menu command.

I create tables of data for our market research department. Is there a way to easily separate columns of data with vertical lines to make them easier to read?

Lines are created in tables by using the vertical bar combined with the Format Tab Set command. By using the Tab command, the vertical bars are aligned properly on every line.

To format the table properly, you must treat it as one paragraph. This means that any hard carriage returns should be replaced with soft carriage returns. The hard carriage return is created by pressing Enter. The soft carriage return is created by pressing Shift + Enter. (If you have the Options menu "show non-printing symbols" field set to "All" or "Partial," a down arrow appears at the end of each line.)

1. Place the cursor in the table, you wish set the vertical lines.

2. Select the Format Tab Set command and press F1.

3. Press the down Arrow and select the Vertical option by pressing V. Press the Up Arrow to return to the Set position command.

4. Press the Right Arrow to move the cursor to the position you would like your first tab. Press Insert to set a vertical line.

If you make a mistake or wish to delete a tab, move the cursor to the desired position on the ruler and press the Delete key.

If the line does not print, select the vertical bar character "|" in the Options "line-draw characters" field.

If I accidently backspace over words that I meant to keep, is there a way to get them back?

By pressing the Undo command, WORD will replace all of the text deleted with the Backspace or Delete key prior to the last pressing of the Enter key or format change.

You may also press Shift + F1 to execute the Undo command.

The Undo command also will undo typing, sorting, and hyphenation.

I can recall seeing a word count at the bottom of the screen but I don't remember how it got there. How can I get a word count of my document?

WORD provides a word count every time a document is printed. If you need to check your word count and don't want to waste paper, use the Print File command to print your document to the file. Set up a regular filename that you will print to so you do not take up unnecessary file space.

When the printing to the file is complete, the line and word count is displayed in the lower left hand corner of the screen. You also may do this with parts of your document using the "selection" field in Print Options menu.

Here is a handy macro for getting the word count:

1. Type the following:

   <esc>PFTEST<enter><enter>Y

2. Select the Copy command.
3. Type COUNT_WORD.MAC^Control+WC and press Enter to Save it.

To execute this macro, Press Ctrl+WC. The macro creates a print file called TEST and subsequently displays the number of words at the bottom of the screen. Pressing any key erases the entry.

Chapter 4

Files

I have several other programs that produce ASCII text files. Can I edit these with Microsoft Word?

WORD will load any ASCII file even though initially you may not see it on the directory. To load the ASCII file, type the full directory, path and filename with the file extension. However, some files may import with hard carriage returns (paragraph marks) at the end of every line. It is a good idea to modify them so the word wrap function can work correctly in WORD.

To replace unwanted paragraph marks, select the Replace command, type ^p in the "text" field and leave the "with" field blank. Confirm each entry so that required paragraph markers remain.

Note: To see all the files in a directory when using a load command, type the path and then add *.*.

I often work with long documents and forget to save my files. Does WORD automatically save my documents?

You can have WORD automatically save your files using the Autosave feature. The Autosave permits the selection of the time interval and whether or not you wish to have the backup confirmed. The style sheet and glossary also are automatically backed up.

Should your computer have a power failure, WORD will prompt you to perform a recovery process upon the restarting of the program. Follow the prompts on the screen.

To initialize the Autosave, select the Options command and enter the time interval in the "autosave" field. If you wish to confirm each save, select "Y" in the "confirm autosave" field.

The Autosave should not take the place of the Transfer Save command because it does not save to the same file. At the end of a work session, you must save the document with the Transfer Save command.

When I display a directory of WORD in DOS, I see a number of files that end in .BAK. Do I need to keep these files?

The BAK files store the previous version of the document, while the files ending in DOC are the current versions. The BAK files are useful for going back to the last edit or for recovering a DOC file that has been lost or damaged.

WORD functions fine without the BAK files, however you should not delete the BAK file of an active document as it may result in loss of that document. When you wish to save space on the disk, removing the BAK files is a good place to start. To remove the BAK files:

1. Clear WORD of any active documents by selecting Transfer Clear All.
2. Select Library Run to execute a DOS command.
3. Type DEL *.BAK and press Enter.
4. Press any key to return to WORD.

Note: This procedure only deletes the BAK files from the selected directory. You must change directories with the Transfer Option command or type the full path name to delete BAK files from other directories.

WORD always comes up with the same directory for the data. Is there a way to change this?

A nice addition to WORD 5.0 is the option to change the default directory when you execute WORD.

1.   Select the Transfer Option command.
2.   Change the name of the Directory and Path to the new name.
3.   Then press the Tab or Down Arrow key to move the cursor to the "save between sessions" field and type Y for Yes.

This feature also is useful for keeping files out of the program directory. (Backups are faster and take up less space if you keep your program files separate from the data files. Since all you need are the data files, back up only the directories with the data files.)

You may still change the default directory during the work session without affecting the default starting directory. To change the default directory for the current session only:

1.   Select the Transfer Option command.
2.   Change the name of the Directory and Path to the new name.

I use many different directories to store my documents. Is there a better way to find the file I am looking for than to type the path name each time?

There are two ways to get around typing the path name each time you wish to load a document.

Upon execution of the Transfer Load command, press F1. A list of the subdirectories and parent directories is displayed. Move the cursor to the one you require and press Enter. The files in the selected directory are displayed. Move the cursor to the desired file and press Enter.

The second way to load the file without typing the file's path name is to use the Transfer Option command and select the new default directory.

There are too many files to be able to find the one I want. How can I better manage my files with WORD?

The best way to manage files is to create a plan before you start to save documents. First, it is a good idea to save all your "once only" documents on a floppy disk instead of the hard drive. Even though it is unlikely you will require them again, you still have an electronic copy should you need it. This helps reduce the clutter on the hard drive and reduces hard drive maintenance procedures. After a disk has been stored for a predetermined amount of time, reformat it and use it again.

As for the rest of the file management, divide the types of writing you do into different categories. Each of these categories is then created as a separate directory. To make a directory called LETTERS while in WORD, select the Library Run command and type MD LETTERS. Now all your letters could be saved to this directory for a more convenient lookup. Each directory you create will automatically display on the file list when you press F1 during a Transfer Load or a Transfer Save.

To find a document easily, it is a good idea to put a description of the document in the summary sheet. This way you can use the Library Document-retrieval command to search for the document. This is a very powerful feature in WORD. To take advantage of it, you must first have the "summary sheet" field set to Yes in the Options menu. Whenever you save a document, fill in the summary sheet with the information you feel you might eventually need to retrieve it.

I see on the screen a "Document Disk Full" message. When I started the document, I estimated the amount of space and it was clear that I had twice as much space available. Why do I get this error and how do I fix it?

WORD requires twice as much file space as the document actually requires. This is because of the backup file created with the BAK extension. There are two alternatives to solve this problem.

The easiest solution is to save to another drive. If you are using a dual floppy system, place another formatted disk in place of the original and select the Transfer Save command. When you see the instructions "Enter Y to retry access to filename.DOC" or "Enter Y to retry access to filename.BAK," insert the original working disk. When you see the prompt "Enter Y to retry access to MWxxxxxx.TMP," insert the new disk.

The other option is to delete .BAK files from the working disk drive. Use the Library Run command to get into DOS. To delete the files, type DEL filename.BAK. Continue to delete files until there is sufficient space to save your working file. Do not delete the BAK file for the current work file. This method is usually faster than the first method but does involve some risk when erasing backup files.

I have a dual floppy laptop. What files do I need to run WORD?

To best run WORD on a laptop, use the SETUP file found on the WORD Utilities disk 1. Type SETUP and follow the instructions on the screen. WORD will determine automatically the correct files with this command.

If you are using 720k or higher capacity drives, the program will fit on one disk, with separate disks for the Speller and Thesaurus. Users of 360k floppies will have two program disks.

To optimize space, limit your selection of printers to only one or two. You can always add or change additional printers by copying the *.PRD files from the printer disks at a later date.

How do I prepare a document with Word to send on a modem?

Preparation of a file for modem transfer is dependent on the type of application required by the receiver and the modem transfer protocol.

If your document is to be used by a receiver who is using WORD, no modification is required. Send the DOC file as you saved it.

If the receiver is using another type of word processor or it is being sent to another type of computer, you will need to send the file as an ASCII character file. An ASCII character file may be prepared two ways.

Some Transfer programs and receivers may require that each line in the document have a carriage return imbedded. To do this, save the file as a "Text-only-with-line-breaks." This option is located in the Transfer Save command by pressing the Down Arrow or Tab key and pressing T twice.

If carriage returns are not required, select the "Text-only" option in the Transfer Save command.

In each case the text files no longer have the format commands required by WORD and can be read by almost any other program that can read a text file.

I've noticed that the number of files with the extension TMP in my WORD directory is growing. How did they get there, what are they for, and do I need them?

The TMP files are "scratch" files that are created by WORD to temporarily store document data. These files are erased by WORD once a document is completed and saved.

Under ideal circumstances, there should not be any TMP files in the directory, except when an active document is being edited. TMP files in the directory are usually a result of not properly exiting WORD using the Quit command. Power failures or other interruptions may also cause the TMP file to remain in the directory.

A TMP file may be used to reconstruct a document should it be lost during a power failure. However, this is not as reliable as using files created by the Autosave feature.

To delete unnecessary TMP files:

1. Clear WORD of any active documents by selecting Transfer Clear All.

2. Select Library Run to execute a DOS command.

3. Type DEL *.TMP and press Enter.

4. Press any key to return to WORD.

Note: This procedure deletes only the TMP files from the selected directory. You must change directories with the Transfer Option command or type the full path name to delete TMP files from other directories.

Chapter 5

Format

Format, Boxes

I like to use a box around lists of special points of interest in my document. However, I get lines drawn between each of the points in the list. How can I eliminate these lines?

Boxes in WORD are formed around a paragraph, using the Format Border Box command. Each time you press the Enter key, a paragraph is formed. When you formatted the list, it consisted of more than one paragraph.

To convert the list to a single paragraph, you must remove the paragraph markers created by the Enter key and replace them with "soft" carriage returns. The soft carriage return is the Shift + Enter keys. If you are displaying the non-printable characters, the Shift + Enter displays as a down arrow symbol.

Note: It is easier to make the above replacements if you are able to see where they are located. To display the non-printable characters, select the Option command. Change the "show non-printing symbols" field to Yes.

My company is creating a small newspaper and would like to be able to start some stories with a two column format, and then switch to a three column format on the same page. How do we do this?

The number of columns on a page is controlled by the Format Division Layout command. In order to have two different column formats on the same page, you have to create a division break and format the new column value below the division break. To have a combination of two and three columns on the same page:

1.   Select Format Division Layout and enter 2 in the "number of columns" field.
2.   Select Continuous in the "division break" field. (This prevents a page break at the division marker.)
3.   Move the cursor to the location where the document is to change from two to three columns.
4.   Press Control + Enter to create a division break.
5.   Select Format Division Layout and enter 2 in the "number of columns" field.
6.   Select Continuous in the "division break" field.

I don't like any of the default margin formats
provided by WORD. Is there a way for me to
change them?

There are several ways to change WORD's
default format settings. Certain selections such
as the Printer Options and the Option command
selections are saved automatically as the defaults
for the next session of WORD and are retained
until a new change is made. Character,
paragraph, and page formats generally are saved
on a style sheet called NORMAL.STY.

Changes to the margin settings may be made
with either a style sheet or by setting to Yes the
"use as default" field in the Format Division
Margin command. To change the default margin
settings:

1. Select the Format, Division, Margin
command.
2. Enter the desired new margin values.
3. Press End to move to the "use as default"
field.
4. Select Yes and press Enter.

Default type fonts may be changed only by
modifying the style sheet NORMAL.STY. To
change the default type fonts:

1. Select the Gallery Insert command.
2. Select Paragraph in the "usage" field.

3. Move to the "variant" field and press F1.

4. Select Paragraph Standard and press Enter.

5. Select the Format Character command.

6. Choose the desired font name and size and press Enter.

7. Select the Transfer Save command and press Enter.

8. Select Exit to leave the Gallery menu.

Our office does not use half inch tabs. Is there a way to change them other than always using the Format Tab option?

The tab default is set up on the Options menu. Select the "default tab width" field and enter the new fractional value.

The Tabs also may be measured in characters using 10 or 12 pitch characters or may be measured in centimeters. Use the "measure" field on the Options menu to make this selection.

If you have unusual Tab settings that are time consuming to set up, you may wish to set them up in a "dummy" document that you load every time you need that particular Tab format. (Save an extra copy just in case you save your document to the dummy file.)

Another option is to create a style sheet with the Tabs formatted. Then attach the style sheet to the document requiring the Tabs. This is a more efficient way to produce the Tabs.

See Measurement in the Beginning section.

Our office makes many forms. They often require that blank lines be drawn. Is there an easier way than using the underline key?

There are a couple of ways to draw lines with WORD. One is with the line drawing feature and the other is with the leading Tab characters.

To draw a line with the line draw feature:

1. Place the cursor where you wish to begin drawing the line.
2. Press Control + F5 to turn line draw on.
3. Use the Arrow keys to draw the line in the direction desired.
4. When the line is complete, press Control + F5 to turn line draw off or press Escape.

Leading Tab characters have a slight advantage over line draw because they are faster to draw and always end up in the same spot. This is particularly useful for repetitive lines that must be aligned. To draw a line with the Tab characters:

1. Select the Format Tab Set command and enter the measurement for the end point of the line.
2. Move to the "leading char." field and select the underscore character. Press Enter.

3. Whenever the Tab key is pressed, a line is drawn from the current cursor position to the point set up as the Tab.

If you wish to save this document and later fill in the form, be sure you are in Overtype mode. Press F5 to switch between Overtype and Insert mode. If you want to keep the data you are entering underlined, be sure to press Alt + XU to turn on the underlining feature.

Some of the type fonts that I select do not appear to make a change in the print out. Why is this happening?

Not all fonts associated with a printer file are available with your printer. You should consult your printer manual for more information on the available or installed fonts.

With laser printers especially, font availability is virtually endless. The font selections showing in WORD's Character "font name" menu may not necessarily correspond to the fonts you have available for your printer.

Because of the wide variety of type fonts and selective needs on the part of users, WORD permits the modification of the PRD file that controls the printer activities. In this file, you may change the name and attributes of fonts available to the printer.

Modifying PRD files can be a somewhat complex task and goes beyond the scope of this book. For an in depth treatment of adding and changing fonts in WORD, see the Printer Information Manual.

Format, Font Selections

After completing my document, I go back and make all the format changes I want. Is there a faster way other than using the Escape Format Character menu selection?

For basic bolding, underlining, and italics, use the speed format keys Alt + B, Alt + U, and Alt + I respectively.

The speed key for selecting type fonts is Alt + F8. The cursor appears in the "font name" field. To change the "font size" field, press the Tab or Right Arrow key.

Another way to speed up the formatting process is to create macros for your most common format procedures. For example, headers in your document may be typed first and later formatted with a macro. To create a macro to apply a larger type style and bolding:

1.   Press Shift + F3 to record a macro. (Every key pressed after this is recorded.)

2.   Press F10 to select a paragraph.

3.   Select the Format Character command and choose the desired formats. For example, set the "bold" field to Yes and the "font size" field to 16. Press Enter.

4.   Press Shift + F3 to turn off Record macro. You are now prompted for the macro name. Type Bold Header ^ Control + H.

To use this macro, simply move the cursor to

the header you wish to format and type Control + H. It will automatically format the line with the desired characteristics you have chosen in the macro.

When I use the footnote option, they all appear at the bottom of the page. How can I get them to appear as endnotes at the end of the document? I also prepare my manuscripts with one file per chapter which is a problem when I want to put the footnotes at the end of the manuscript.

Footnote control in WORD is a bit obscure. It is located in the Format Layout command menu. To change the footnote location, select either Same-page or End in the "footnote" field.

If your manuscript consists of many files, the footnotes are at the end of each file. To place them at the end of the manuscript, you must first merge all of the files into one large file. WORD then renumbers the footnotes. To merge the files:

1. Press Control + PageDown to go to the end of the first file.
2. Select the Transfer Merge command to load in the next document.
3. Type the document name or press F1 and select from the list.
4. Repeat steps 1-3 until all the documents are merged.

When I format a paragraph to have the first line flush with the left margin and the rest of the paragraph indented, the entire paragraph is indented. How can I get the first line to be flush with left margin?

To indent all but the first line of a paragraph you must format the first line with a negative number. The negative number should be the inverse of the value used for the indent. To create a hanging indent of 1 inch, do the following steps:

1. Select Format Paragraph.
2. Move the cursor to the "left indent" field and enter 1.
3. Move the cursor to the "first line" field and enter -1. Press Enter.

There is also a speed format key which will use the default tab settings for the Hanging Paragraph. Press Alt + T (or Alt + XT) to execute this command.

We'd like to create instructions for clerks filling out forms with Word, however, we do not want the instructions printed.

To create text on a form for operator use only, use the hidden text feature of WORD. There are several ways to format hidden text. Using the menu command:

1. Highlight the text.
2. Select the Format Character command.
3. Change the "hidden" field to Yes.

Using the speed format keys:

1. Highlight the text.
2. Press Alt + E (Alt + XE).

During text entry:

1. Press Alt + E (Alt + XE).
2. Type the text that is to appear hidden.
3. Press Alt + Spacebar.

If the text disappears, you are probably in the "show layout" mode. See if an LY is displayed in the status line at the bottom of the screen. If it is, select the Options command and change the "show layout" field to No.

I have a list of projects in a document and I would like to have flush left and right margins. The Justify command does not seem to work. What do I do?

WORD automatically spaces out all the lines of a justified paragraph except the last line. This prevents a short last line from looking strange from all the added spaces. Because of this, a single line paragraph is not justified.

There is a way around this problem. By using the "soft" carriage return, Shift + Enter, the lines in a list are treated by WORD as one paragraph. Each sentence is on a separate line but now is justified.

To justify a paragraph, select Format Paragraph and choose Justified in the "alignment" field. You is also may use the speed format key Alt + XJ or Alt + J.

I printed a document that was printed in Version 4.0 on my laser printer and the margin is different than the print out that was made in version 5.0.

WORD 4.0 did not properly account for the unprintable portions of the paper. This resulted in many users having to alter the margin dimensions to compensate for document misalignment.

WORD 5.0 accounts for the unprintable portions of the paper so that all margins print accurately. This means that a document created in WORD 4.0 will not align the same way in 5.0.

To correct the alignment, select the Format Division Margin command and revise the margin measurements. You also may want to change the default margins. This is done by changing the "use as default" to Yes in the Format Division command menu.

Can I automatically number lines and paragraphs?

Numbering in WORD can be done easily by creating a glossary command to simplify the numbering process. WORD does automatic numbering by using a code that you create in front of the paragraphs or lines to be numbered. The code consists of text followed by a colon. To distinguish the code from body text, you must press F3 after entering the colon. This places the code in parentheses. The following example demonstrates how this works:

1. At the beginning of the line you wish to number, type no: (short for number) and press F3. The numbering code is now created.

2. To convert this to a glossary, highlight the newly created code (no:) and select the Copy command. Type N to save the numbering code as a one letter glossary.

3. In front of every line or paragraph you want to number, type N and press F3. The (no:) code is placed in front of the line. A list of items would appear as follows:

(no:) Item A
(no:) Item B
(no:) Item C
(no:) Item D

The printout correctly numbers the list as follows:

1 Item A
2 Item B
3 Item C
4 Item D

Use the Print preView command to preview the numbering on the screen.

When I format a document for my printer, the page numbers are sometimes printed in a different type font. How can I get my page numbers to print in the same type font as my body text?

The font selection for page numbers may be changed with either of two different methods. If you are using the Format Division Page-number command to print the page numbers, the font for the page number must be changed on the style sheet. To change the default font:

1. Select the Gallery Insert command.
2. Move the cursor to the variant field. Press F1, select Page Number, and press Enter.
3. Select the Format command and make the desired Font (or other format) selections. Press enter when all the changes have been completed.

You also can print page numbers using Running Heads. A Running Head is text that is printed in the top or bottom margins of the document. By formatting the Running Head with the Format Character command, you have absolute control over the page number format. To create and format a page number at the bottom right hand corner of the document with a running head:

1. Create the (page) macro by typing page and pressing F3.

2. Press F10 to highlight (page). Select Format Character and apply the appropriate formatting.

3. Press Alt + R, (Alt + XR), to right justify the page.

4. Select Format Running-head Bottom and press Enter.

5. Select Format Division Margins and enter .5 in the running-head field, "from bottom," to indicate printing half an inch from the bottom of the page.

6. Press Enter.

We have to fill in a great deal of forms in the office. Because we rely heavily on word processing instead of typewriters, filling in forms can be very tedious. What is the best way to use WORD to fill out preprinted forms?

Filling out forms with WORD is very easy once you have built the form as a document. There are three components to building the document to fill out a preprinted form. First, you must create the list of entries to be filled in and label them. Second, you hide the labels so they don't print. Finally, you position the entries so they print in the proper place on the form. Follow these steps to build a document to fill in a form:

1. Type a label for each entry for the form. The label should be information to assist in filling out the form. At the end of the label entry, press Control +]. This produces a chevron symbol, ">>", at the end of the label.

2. Highlight the label and chevron for each entry and press Alt + E twice (Alt + XE if you have a style sheet attached). This converts the label to hidden text. If the text is not displaying on the screen, check to see the Options menu "show layout" field is set to No and the "show hidden text" is set to Yes.

3. Measure the location from the left and

top of the form for the starting character for each entry on the preprinted form.

4. Select Format pOsition for each entry. Enter the location in inches from the left side of the page to the "horizontal frame position" field and from the top of the page in the "vertical frame position." Set the "relative to" fields to Page.

5. Save the document with the Transfer Save command.

I've created a running head in my document, but it doesn't print. What causes this?

A running head is used to place information in the top or bottom margin of a document and is often used for page numbers and document information.

Running heads are positioned and measured relative to the edge of the paper and not the top margin. If the position of the running head is measured to a location in the body of the text, it will not print.

To alter the location of the running head:

1. Select the Format Division Margin command.

2. Enter the measurement in the "running-head position from top:" field or "from bottom" field depending on the location.

Another possible cause of unprinted running heads may be the even or odd pages field being turned off. Select the Format Running-head command and make sure the "even" and "odd" fields are set to yes.

When I create a running head, it disappears off the screen. How can I later edit it?

The running head disappears if the display is in the show layout mode. To show the running head:

1. Select the Options command.
2. Choose the "show layout" field and select No. The running head will reappear.

The running head does not print as you see it on the screen. It is printed in the top or bottom margin according to the values set in the Format Division menu.

Running heads also may have their position controlled relative to the left margin or to the edge of the paper. This selection is made in the Format Running-head menu.

Sometimes I bold single characters using the speed format keys and nothing happens. Other times the formatting goes all the way to the end of the document. Why?

The same command is used by WORD to turn on text format and to format existing text. This results in both of the above problems occurring.

The Alt key is used to speed format text with keys such as B for Bold, I for Italics and U for underline. Alt + B would turn on the bold feature. (If a style sheet is attached, an X must be added to the command, e.g. Alt +XB.) If no text is highlighted, the format is presumed to be turned on. When the Alt + Spacebar is pressed, the formatting is turned off. If you do not press the Alt + spacebar, the formatting continues to the end of the document.

Single character formatting requires that the speed formatting be entered twice. This is because one entry of the speed key turns the feature on if only one character is highlighted. You can get around this if the single character you are formatting is followed by a space. Press F7 or F8 to highlight the character along with the space. The desired format command then is selected only once.

I frequently need to change my tabs in documents. Can WORD let me enter tabs in inches?

If the tab changes are uniform, the quickest solution is to select the Options menu and change the "default tab width" field to the desired new value.

Tab sets are associated with the paragraph(s) they are written with. Provided you do not delete the paragraph marker, each paragraph may be formatted separately.

Select the Format Tab Set command and press F1. The measurement is displayed and Tabs may be entered by pressing the arrow keys and selecting a location with the Insert command.

You also may use the speed format keys Alt + F1. Press Alt + F1 and enter the value of your tab in inches. In order for the ruler to display, select the Options command and change the "show ruler" field to Yes.

Chapter 6

Graphics

Graphics, Block Letters

Our church bulletin has a summary of the sermon that starts with a big block letter. What commands in Word can I use to make this possible?

You can add a large block letter to the beginning of a document either by typing the text or by importing a graphic. To format the letter into the document:

1. Place the letter or graphic in the line just above the body of the text.
2. Highlight the paragraph or place the cursor over the letter.
3. Select the Format Character command to change the font size, select italics, bold, or any other formats.

4. If a box is desired, select the Format Border Box command.

5. Select the Format pOsition command to locate the graphic. Accept the default positions. The "width" field is the only one that needs to be changed to reflect the width of the frame containing the letter. If you need more space between the letter and the text body, change the "distance from text" field. Press Enter when finished.

In our annual reports, we have charts imported from Excel. How can we put descriptive captions under our chart?

If your chart does not have a border around it:

1.   Place the cursor at the end of the graphic and press Enter.
2.   Type the caption.

If your chart does have a border around it:

1.   Place the cursor at the end of the graphic and press Shift + Enter.
2.   Type the caption.

Note: You may optionally format the caption with the Format Character command. The caption may be as many lines as you need. Press Shift + Enter between lines of the caption.

Our company is creating its own software documentation. Is there an easy way to import the screens from the software in the documentation?

WORD has a special utility program called CAPTURE.COM. If it is not already on your word directory, copy it from Utilities disk 3. Set up CAPTURE.COM by typing CAPTURE/s and select the appropriate options.

To capture a screen:

1. Load CAPTURE if it is not already loaded. The program resides in memory and you now can load your application.

2. To capture a screen, press Shift + Printscreen.

3. A filename is displayed at the top of the screen. Accept this name or change it to one of your choice. The extension .SCR is added if it is a graphics screen and .LST if it is a text screen. If you have saved the file as a text file, the process is complete.

4. If you chose a graphics format, you may edit the screen as outlined in Chapter 22 of the Microsoft WORD manual. Press Enter when finished to complete the screen save.

5. A beep sounds when the process is complete.

Use the Library Link Graphics command in WORD to import the screen.

Note: Graphics cannot be modified once they have been imported.

What does the term "Frames" mean in Word?

Frames are used by WORD to hold a specific graphic. A frame is positioned in the document, indicating where the graphic will be placed. By selecting the "show layout" field as "Yes," you can see the positioning of the frame in the document. The graphic does not appear in the frame, however. If you wish to see the graphic in place, select the Print preView command.

Controlling the frame width affects the placement of text around it. By changing the "width" and the "distance from text" fields in the Format pOsition command, you change the look of the text relative to the graphic.

I'm creating a newsletter and would like to incorporate a graph created in Lotus. What steps do I take to incorporate the graph?

Lotus graphs must first be saved as Lotus PIC files. (A PIC file is a specific graphic format that must be communicated to WORD during the import process.) For convenience, save them or transfer them to the WORD directory. To import the file into your document:

1.   Place the cursor in the position you wish to place the graph.
2.   Select the Library Link Graphics command.
3.   Enter the filename of the PIC file.
4.   If the "file format" field is blank, type PIC.
5.   Change the "width" and "height" fields if desired.
6.   Add additional white space above and below the graphic with the "space before" and "space after" fields.
7.   Press Enter to import the graphic.

If you wish to reposition the graphic in your document, highlight it and use the Format pOsition command.

Graphics, Line Drawing

I'm trying to create an organizational chart, but I can get only one box on a line. How do I get more boxes on the line?

To create more than one box on a line, do not use the Format Border Box feature. Instead, use the line drawing feature. To draw lines:

1. Move the cursor to the position you wish to begin drawing a line or box.
2. Press Control + F5 to turn on the line draw feature.
3. Use the Arrow keys to draw the lines.
4. When the drawing is complete, press Esc.

If you wish to change the line draw character, select the Options menu and press F1 in the "linedraw character" field. Some printers cannot print certain characters so you may wish to test them.

To add text inside a box created with the line draw feature, you must switch to overtype mode by pressing F5. The initials OT are displayed on the status line.

My printer is not producing graphics. Is there a way to correct this?

First make sure your printer is capable of printing in a graphics mode. If only part of a graphic prints on a laser printer, you may have insufficient memory in the printer.

Next check to be sure you have imported the graphic correctly and the right format was used in the Library Link Graphic command. To be sure the graphic is being acknowledged by WORD, try the Print preView to see if the graphic is actually there.

There is one last thing to check if everything else is in order. Check to see if the Print Options menu "draft" field is set to Yes. If it is, change it to No. This could correct the problem because the draft option turns off the microjustification feature of many printers. With this feature turned off, most graphics cannot be printed.

I've seen documents that have boxes for shading in it. Can you do this with WORD?

Your printer must be able to support shading in order for you to shade a box. To check if your printer supports this feature, select Format Border Box and place the cursor in the "background shading" field. Press F1 to view options. If your printer is not supported, a message stating that this is the case will be displayed. To shade a box, assuming your printer supports it:

1. Select the Format Borders Box command.
2. Move the cursor to the "background shading" field and select a number from 1 to 100 or press F1 to see the selections. (1 is the lightest and 100 is the darkest.)
3. Press Enter to accept the selections.

In our newsletter, we wanted to make the chart smaller than its original size when it was created. How do we make a size difference?

WORD can change the relative size of a graphic by fitting the imported graphic to a frame you have created. WORD cannot directly alter the amount of the graphic displayed or "crop" it. Cropping can be done, however, if the CAPTURE utility is used.

Sizing is accomplished as a part of the Library Link Graphics command. When this command is executed, enter the dimensions in the "graphics width" field. The height field will be calculated proportionally. If you want to override the automatic calculation of the height field, enter the desired value.

If you are capturing a screen graphic using the CAPTURE.COM utility, you may crop the graphic before completing the capture. This helps provide a precise fit when used with the Library Link Graphics options.

See Chapter 22 in the Microsoft WORD manual for more details on using CAPTURE.

Our school newspaper requires a vertical line between every column. How are these vertical lines inserted into the lay out?

The simplest way to add lines between newspaper style columns is to set the space between columns to 0 and use the Format Border Line command to create the lines. Follow these steps:

1. Select the Format Division Layout command.

2. Enter the number of columns desired in the "number of columns" field.

3. Enter 0 in the "space between columns" field.

4. Press Enter.

5. Highlight all the areas in which you wish to have the lines.

6. Select the Format Border Lines command.

7. Choose Yes in the fields "left" and "right."

8. Press Enter to complete the formatting.

This results in borders between and outside all of the columns.

Chapter 7

Macros and Glossaries

Macros and Glossaries, Applications and Definition

What is the difference between a macro and a glossary?

A glossary is text stored in an abbreviated form. It can be used to store entries such as common names, addresses, letter closings, text with complex formatting and special characters.

A macro is a glossary with more options. With a macro, you may add menu and other WORD commands. Macros are saved similarly to glossaries. They often are named with control codes (Control plus 1 or 2 letters) for fast execution. Use macros to change formats, insert information, create tables, find a document or run operating system commands. Whenever you find yourself repeating keystrokes unnecessarily, consider a macro.

Entering commands to create a macro require using the less than "<" and greater than ">" signs around the macro command. For example, the following macro would be typed to bold a line and then search for the word "format."

<home><f6><end><alt   X><alt
B><esc>sformat<enter>

To save this macro:

1.   Press F6 and the arrow keys to highlight it.

2.   Select the Copy command.   Type the macro name, a caret, "^", and Control + S (or any desired key).

To execute the macro, press Control + S.

In preparing documents, I have words that are repeated frequently in the document. How can I reduce the number of keystrokes repeated?

To reduce text keystrokes in WORD, you create a glossary. Follow these steps:

1. Type the text you wish to repeat.
2. Highlight the text to be entered. (If you have just typed the text, hold the Shift key and press the left arrow.)
3. Select the Copy command.
4. Type the abbreviated command you wish to use to recall the macro. Press Enter.

To use a glossary, type the abbreviation as it was created and press F3.

The glossary is saved only if you respond Yes to the save glossaries prompt when you quit WORD.

Is there an easier way to delete a list of macros than one at a time?

WORD deletes macros with the Transfer Glossary Clear command. To delete multiple glossaries at the same time:

1. Select Transfer Glossary Clear.
2. Press F1 and choose the first macro to be deleted. (Do not press Enter.)
3. Type a comma.
4. Repeat steps 2 and 3 until all the glossaries to be deleted are listed.
5. Press Enter to delete the list.

If you find it easier to work from a printed copy, use the Print Glossary command.

After creating a macro, I have discovered that it doesn't work the way I want it to. How do I edit it?

When preparing a macro, it is inevitable that an error will be made. Editing the macro is an easy task.

1. Type the macro name followed by the caret "^" symbol.
2. Press F3 and the macro text is inserted into the document.
3. Edit the text.
4. Highlight the glossary or macro.
5. Select the Copy command and type the name with which you wish to save it.
6. Press Enter.

If you can't remember the name of the macro you wish to edit:

1. Select the Insert command.
2. Press F1 to see the list.
3. Point to the desired macro.
4. Type the caret "^" symbol and press Enter.

I've created a macro to search for paragraph markers. When I do the search manually, the paragraph markers are found. When I use a macro, the paragraph markers are not found.

When searching for a format character, you must add an extra caret, "^", to the macro. For example, when searching for the paragraph marker, you would use the ^P in the Search command. To fulfil the same function in a macro use ^^P.

To create a macro to search for the ^P paragraph marker:

1. Type <esc>s^^p.
2. Highlight the entry.
3. Select the copy command.
4. Type SearchP^ and press Control + P.

To search for the paragraph symbol, type Control P.

I tried to use one of the macros supplied by WORD, but it did not work. How can I get it to work?

There are several glossary files with WORD. The one that is available when you start WORD is called NORMAL.GLY. The supplied macros with WORD are in a glossary called MACRO.GLY. To load it:

1. Select the Transfer Glossary Load command.

2. Type MACRO and press Enter. (Note: If you are not in the WORD directory, you must type the full path name C:\WORD5\MACRO.)

If you wish to avoid this step every time you require a supplied macro, you need to merge the MACRO.GLY glossary with the default or NORMAL.GLY glossary. To merge the two glossaries:

1. Select the Transfer Glossary Merge command.

2. Type C:\WORD5\MACRO.

If you wish to replace the merged NORMAL.GLY with the original NORMAL.GLY, you will have to copy it from the original distribution disk.

Am I limited to only 26 letters to name macros?

Macros may be executed using either the Control key plus one or two characters or with a macro name. A macro name may be up to 31 characters long.

If you choose to use long names for your macros, it is easiest to execute them using the Insert command, pressing F1 and selecting them from the list.

Select Control characters that make sense to you. For example, to bold a header, you may use the command Control + BH.

To avoid confusion in searching for macros versus glossaries, you may wish to add the characters "mac" to the macro name. To make using glossaries efficient, try to limit the number of letters used in the name.

I created a glossary during a prior session using Word. When I attempt to use the glossary I created, nothing happens.

A glossary that doesn't function may be the result of a failure to save it. Another possible explanation for failure is that it was saved in another macro glossary.

Glossaries that are created during a session of WORD and not manually saved must be saved at the end of the WORD session. The save is prompted when you select the Quit command. If you respond with a Y, the glossaries are saved.

Macros and Glossaries also may be saved using the Transfer Glossary Save command. Press Enter to save them to the current glossary or change to the glossary desired.

A glossary that doesn't execute also may be a result of having the wrong glossary file loaded. To change the current glossary file, select the Transfer Glossary Load command. Press F1 to see the options. Select a glossary and press Enter. Repeat this process until you find your macro.

Chapter 8

Merging

Merging, Applications and Definition

How does Word's mail merge work, and what uses besides a mail merge are there?

Applications for the merging feature include, labels, form letters, specialized forms, invoices, contracts, personnel and other types of application forms, and memos.

A WORD mail merge consists of two documents. There is a main document and a data document. The main document might be a letter to customers that contains the merge instructions. The data document stores the information to placed in the appropriate fields of the main document.

The main document must have a DATA instruction as the first line of the document to indicate the name of the data document. If the name of the data document is LIST.DOC, the data statement would read <<DATA

LIST.DOC>>.

Each field that is to have data merged to it is identified by the chevrons. The chevrons are created by pressing Control plus the open "[" or close "]" square brackets.

A letter for a mail merge might appear as follows:

```
<<DATA LIST.DOC>>

<<Name>>
<<Address>>
<<City>>,<<ST>>    <<ZIP>>

Dear <<Name>>:

Thank you for your past business.
We look forward to serving you this
year.  Feel free to call us for
assistance.

Sincerely,
```

The data document consists of a first line that labels each of the fields in the data document. Each field name is separated with a comma. Each line in the data document is one record with the field order matching the first line field name line. The field names must match those used in the document. The following example could be the contents of LIST.DOC.

```
Name,Address,City,ST,ZIP
Bill Smith,123 Any Street,New York,NY,10007
John Jones,P.O. Box 1234,Los Angelos,CA,94565
```

Use the Print Merge Print command while in the main document to produce the merge.

How do I prepare addresses from a non-WORD mailing list for a WORD mail merge list?

For a mailing list to merge correctly, it must be formatted so the main document it will be merged with can read it properly. The format consists of adding a line at the beginning of the data file that indicates the names of each field. Each record of data then is maintained on a single line in the order prescribed by the first line of the file. Each field within the record is separated with a comma.

The mailing list then is imported into WORD with the Transfer Load command. The modified file should appear something like the following example:

```
Name,Address,City,ST,ZIP
Bill Smith,123 Any Street,New York,NY,10007
John Jones,P.O. Box 1234,Los Angelos,CA,94565
```

Because many mailing lists place each field on a separate line, you may have to do some editing before the list is useable. This may be done quickly by creating a macro.

We frequently send a standard thank you letter to our customers. We like to customize it for the product the customer ordered. What is the best way to create a form letter in which data frequently changes?

A form letter for frequently changed data is a good candidate for the ASK command. The document is created first, and each item of text to be changed is entered as a merge field. To create a merge field:

1. Type a Control + [.
2. Type the field name you wish to use, i.e. product.
3. Type a Control +].

The merge field will appear surrounded with two chevrons, e.g., <<product>>.

At the beginning of the document, an ASK statement is used to prompt the operator to enter the data. The ASK statement is created with the following steps:

1. Press Control + [.
2. Type ASK fieldname=?message.
3. Type Control +].

For example, to prompt for a product name, the ASK statement would be:
<<ASK product=?Enter product name>>.

To use the ask routine with multiple documents, select the Print Merge command. Each ASK prompt will be displayed and will wait for an entry before printing the document.

When doing a mail merge, sometimes we get a blank set of data. How can we correct this?

Blank data fields are caused by empty records. Load the mail merge file and scan it for empty lines. Then delete the extra blank lines.

One way to make your merge process more effective is to load the main document and data document into two separate windows. This way you may inspect the mailing list easily every time an error occurs. On a large mailing list, you should take the extra time to insure an accurate list.

This method of running the mail merge has an additional benefit because records printed before an error occurred can be temporarily deleted. The merge can be restarted without duplicate documents. (Make sure you have an extra copy of the data file before making deletions.)

To create the separate windows:

1. Select the Windows Split Horizontal command.
2. Type 10 in the "at line" field.
3. Tab to the "clear new window" field and select Yes. Press Enter.
4. Load the data file with the Transfer Load command.
5. Press F1 and load the main document into the first window.

When I execute the Print Merge command, nothing happens. What are the possible errors that may have occurred?

The first thing to check is the DATA statement at the beginning of your document. If it does not exist on the main document, there is no data selected. If there is a DATA statement, be sure the file that is being called is a valid file. (You can test this by seeing if the file loads correctly using the Transfer Load command.)

The next major source of error is a missing or incorrect field description line in the data document. Load the data document and check to see that the field description line appears as the first line. Each field should be separated with a comma and there should be no spaces between field names. This syntax also should be consistent in the rest of the data lines.

Check each of the field names in the field description line and make sure they are spelled the same way as in the main document. This is accomplished easily by opening a second window and loading the data document.

Check for extra commas in a record, because this results in the fields shifting to the wrong location in the main document.

Be sure all the field names in the main document are enclosed in chevrons. These are created by pressing Control plus the open "[" or close "]" square brackets.

Our company takes phone requests for product literature. We would like to use Word to enter the data, and then create mailing labels at the end of the day for mailing requests.

To create mailing labels, you must have two documents. The main document contains the format information for the mailing label. The data document contains the data that will be printed on the label.

In this example, the data document contains all the information about the customer and the particular product information they are requesting. Each record is typed on a separate line. Because the data must be consistent, a header line describing the fields is placed at the top of the data document. This header line describes each of the fields in the data document. For example:

```
name,address,city,ST,ZIP,literature
Bill Smith,123 Any Street,New York,NY,10007,lamps
John Jones,P.O. Box 1234,LA,CA,94565,furniture
```

The field called literature is not actually printed on the label but is used to identify the requested items. At the end of the day, the data document is printed to provide the item information. This file is saved to a file called LBLDATA.

The mailing label is set up in a document called LABEL. To create the mailing label main document, type the following:

<<DATA LBLDATA.DOC>><<name>>
<<address>>
<<city>>, <<ST>>   <<ZIP>>

    To create the open chevron, press Control +
[. To create the closed chevron press Control +
].
To format the label for printing, you must change
the page length and margins of the division so
that one label is considered to be one page. For
a 15/16 inch or 1 inch label, use page length of 1.
Set top and bottom margins to 0 and set the left
margin to .5 inch. With the main document
called LABEL loaded, select the Print, Merge,
Printer command. The labels are printed.

We would like to send price quotes for certain product lines based on location of the customer. What steps, using the mail merge feature, will it take to do this?

To do selective merging of large amounts of data, as in a price list, you use two special commands. One is the INCLUDE command and the other is the IF command.

The IF command provides the decision criteria for selecting the merge data and the INCLUDE command merges the appropriate data. The IF command checks a predetermined data field, such as a ZIP code field, from the mail merge data file. Each IF statement must be concluded with an ENDIF statement. The INCLUDE command merges the text from the file indicated in the INCLUDE statement.

To create a series of price lists based on a customer's zip code:

Start with a main document that includes all the appropriate criteria for a mail merge. In the location where the price lines are to be placed, enter the following:

```
<<IF ZIP>0 and ZIP<10000>><<INCLUDE
PRICE1.DOC>><<ENDIF>>
<<IF ZIP>9999 and ZIP<20000>><<INCLUDE
PRICE2.DOC>><<ENDIF>>
<<IF ZIP>1999 and ZIP<30000>><<INCLUDE
PRICE3.DOC>><<ENDIF>>
```

To create the chevron characters:
1. Press Control + [for the open chevron.
2. Press Control +] for the close chevron.

Chapter 9

Outline

Outline, Applications

What are the benefits of using the WORD outlining feature?

Creating an outline for your document is a unique feature of WORD. The outlining function of WORD is actually an integrated part of the document it outlines. Each of the headings in the outline is a heading in the document. The power is in the ability to reorganize the document easily by moving just the outline headers. The text associated with the header is automatically moved with it.

Using the outline mode, you can quickly scroll to any point in your document, then return to document mode. This is a very useful feature in a large document.

The outline also may become your table of contents by using the Library Table command. (More on using the outline as a Table in the section on Tables and Indexes.)

A very effective way to use the outline mode is by having your document repeated in a second window. In one window you would have the document displayed in the text mode and in the other, in outline mode. To do this:

1. Select the Transfer Window Horizontal command.

2. Choose No in the "clear new window" field.

3. Press Shift + F2 to display the outline in the new window.

How do I coordinate the document text with the outline?

Body text can be added either in the outline edit mode or in the document mode. To enter text in the document mode, place the cursor under the appropriate heading and begin typing.

To add text in outline edit mode, check first to be sure you are in outline edit mode. Change from document mode by pressing Shift + F2. Switch from outline organize mode by pressing Shift + F5. To add the text:

1. Place the cursor at the end of the heading where the body text will follow.
2. Press Enter.
3. Press Alt + P (Alt + XP).
4. Type the text.

I'm trying to figure out how to create sublevels in my outline and how to have them numbered automatically.

Levels of the outline are controlled by pressing Alt + 0 to lower the heading level and Alt + 9 to raise it. Each lower level is indented to the right.

To number the outline:

1. Move the cursor to the beginning of the outline.

2. Select the outline view mode by pressing Shift + F2.

3. Select the Library Number command.

4. Select Update.

5. Select Yes in the "restart sequence" field.

6. Press Enter.

If you modify the outline, you repeat the numbering sequence to reflect the change.

Note: WORD recognizes numbering systems using Arabic or Roman numerals. You may also use letters or legal numbers (1,1.1,1.2,...). Make sure a space, period or closed parenthesis shows the end of the number entry.

Can I outline an existing document?

To create an outline from an existing document, edit the document to show headers or paragraphs that will identify the appropriate levels of the outline. Then:

1. Press Shift + F2 to switch to Outline View mode.
2. Locate the cursor in each paragraph to be a heading and press Alt + 9.
3. After all the headings have been entered, select each heading that is to be indented or changed to a lower level and press Alt + 0.

Chapter 10

Printer

Printer, Back to Back Printing

My printer does not support printing documents on both sides of the paper. Is there a way that WORD can do this for me?

WORD can print selective pages of a document. To print back to back, you must print all the odd number pages in one run. Then place the odd pages back in the printer, upside down, and print the even pages on them. To do this:

1. Select the Print Options command.
2. Go to the "range" field and select Pages.
3. Go to the "page numbers" field and enter the odd page numbers of the document, separated by commas.
4. Print the document.
5. Select the Print Options command.

6.   Go to the "page numbers" field and enter the even page numbers of the document, separated by commas.

7.   Place the printed document back in the printer with the first page on top and face down.

8.   Repeat the print command.

If you have to print the same document frequently, create a macro to enter the page numbers.

How do I get bullets to appear in my document?

Bullets are a function of the printer's capability to print them. Check your printer manual for a list of the characters it can print. If you do not know whether your printer can print them, you can experiment with several characters in the Extended character set.

To display the extended characters on your monitor, hold down the Alt key and type the number code on the numeric keypad.

A small round bullet may be printed with Alt + 249. A small square bullet is Alt + 254. The diamond is Alt + 4. A right pointing arrow is available with Alt + 16.

A bulleted list can be created automatically using the "bullet_list.mac" macro. The list uses a hyphen as the bullet, however, you could modify the macro to use any of the above suggested bullets. To use this macro:

1. Select the Transfer Glossary Load command.
2. Press F1 and highlight MACRO.GLY in the C:\WORD5 directory.
3. Press Enter.
4. Select the Insert command.
5. Press F1 and highlight the bullet_list.mac macro.
6. Press Enter to execute the macro.

I've been using a dot matrix printer and recently purchased a laser printer. What changes should I expect to make for my document to print correctly?

The major issues to be concerned with when changing printers are the type fonts and formatting of the document. WORD carries the bolding, underlining, and italics formatting automatically, and provided the printer supports these features, there should be no loss of format. WORD also attempts to choose the closest available font to the previous printer in use. Follow these setups to insure your document prints the way you desire:

1. Check character fonts by pressing Alt + F8. If the whole document is done in the same font, press shift + F10, then press Alt + F8. Press F1 to select the font choices. Then press TAB and F1 to select the font size.

2. Check the margins with the Format division Margin command. Although they are still the same, you may wish to change the appearance of the document due to font changes. (The font size may take more or less space, thereby requiring resizing the document.)

3. Check Pagination with the Printer Repaginate command.

During the course of the week, I make several revisions of a document. I'd like to print the date it was revised. How can I date stamp the document?

Dates may be automated two different ways with glossaries supplied by WORD. To display the current date on the screen:

1. Type date.
2. Press F3. The date is displayed automatically.

If an incorrect date displays, you must go to DOS to reset it. To do this:

1. Select the Library Run command.
2. Type DATE and press Enter.
3. WORD then exits to DOS and executes the date function. Enter the new date and press Enter. You are returned to WORD.

The disadvantage to the DATE macro is it must be reentered each time the date changes. The DATEPRINT macro, however, prints the current date every time the document is printed. To insert DATEPRINT in your document:

1. Type DATEPRINT.
2. Press F3. (dateprint) is displayed in parentheses.

Note: If the DATE or DATEPRINT macro do not function, check to see the original NORMAL.GLY glossary is loaded.

When I select the draft mode option on the print options menu, the document does not appear to print any differently. How can I get a draft mode print out?

When you select the draft mode in the Printer Options menu, the only change made is that the micro-justification feature is disabled. As a result printer speed is optimized slightly. Near letter quality or font changes are not turned off, however, so the printer does not actually print in a true draft mode.

Because the micro-justification feature is disabled, paragraphs that are justified may not appear justified in the printout. In addition, graphics will not print.

To get a true draft mode printout on a dot matrix printer, select the TTY printer option with the Print Options command. If you do not see this selection, copy the TTY.PRD file from your printer disk.

Note: If your printer has just been printing in near letter quality, you may need to turn it off and on to reset it for draft mode.

Preparing envelopes without a typewriter is very inconvenient. Is there an easier way with Word?

The procedure for printing envelopes is dependent on the type of printer being used. For a dot matrix printer:

1. Select the Format Division Margin command.
2. Set the top margin to 0. Set the left margin to 4 inches. Press Enter.
3. Place the envelope in the printer with the print head aligned one line above where the address is to begin.
4. You may wish to save the address format for future use with the Transfer Save command.
5. Type the address.
6. Select the Print Printer command and press Enter.

Because of the many different ways that laser printers handle envelopes, you will have to experiment to get the correct results. Here are some tips.

1. Many laser printers will not take a No. 10 envelope fed like a regular letter in the portrait orientation. Instead it must be fed, rotated 90 degrees, in a landscape orientation. The landscape orientation requires the printer selection be changed on the Print Options menu.

In addition, you must change the page length and width values to reflect the rotation of the paper and the size of the envelope. Use the Format Division Margins menu to change the dimensions.

2. Depending on the positioning of the envelope, you may have to radically alter the top and left margins. If the feeder positions the envelope to the top of a normal page, use 2 inches as a starting point. If in the middle, try 4 inches and at the bottom, try 6 inches. Set the left margin for 4 inches.

3. Change the "paper feed" field to manual if you are using a single sheet feeder.

Note: Printing envelopes is a good procedure to turn into a macro once you have determined the correct procedure for your printer.

The top of the first page in my printed document has an extra blank line. How do I eliminate it?

This is a feature change between WORD 4.0 and WORD 5.0. WORD 4.0 did not calculate the spacing of the first line and began printing at the location of the printhead. WORD 5.0 calculates the top margin and the line spacing of the first line.

This is important to know for creating forms and having them align properly. As it initially seems logical to align the print head where you want to start printing, the result is an apparent extra blank line.

Form alignment should take this into consideration. To compensate properly, be sure to align the top of the form so it is precisely below the print head. It should be positioned so one line feed would place the printhead on the first line.

___

Hidden text is showing up on my print out. How do I eliminate it?

Hidden text may be showing in your print out for a couple of reasons:

First, be sure the text that is printing actually is hidden. To check this, place the cursor in the location of the hidden text. Select the Format Character command and check the "hidden text" field to see if it says Yes. If not:

1. Highlight the text.
2. Press Alt + E (Alt + XE) or select the Format Character command and change the "hidden text" field to Yes.

Second, check the Print Options screen. The "hidden text" field should be set to No.

If you do not see the hidden text on your screen, check to see if you are in show layout mode. If you are, an "LY" will appear at the bottom of the screen. Also check the Options screen to see if you have the "show hidden text" field set to No.

I would like to use character formatting provided by my printer but not available in the font selection menu. Is there a way to do this without modifying the printer PRD file?

If your printer is not supported by WORD or special features are not available, you can imbed special characters in you document to accomplish the desired formatting. The characters you imbed in the document are referred to as printer control commands or Escape commands. You will have to experiment as some commands may not work.

Most printers require an ASCII code 27 to start a control command. Printers all vary in what commands are used for a specific format type. You first will need to review your printer manual for more details on what the codes are.

For example, to print expanded characters on a Star printer, you might use the codes 27, 87, and 49. To enter this in the document, you would press Alt + 27, Alt + 87, and Alt + 49. To cancel the expanded characters, the codes would be 27, 87, and 48.

The screen will display ASCII characters that correspond to the symbols in the IBM extended character set. These characters generally will not be recognized by your printer as printable characters.

Nothing is printed. What do I do?

There are a number of reasons that your document is not printing. If you get a "Printer is not Ready," "Press Y to continue or Esc to cancel," message or nothing happens, check the following:

1. Be sure the printer is plugged in and turned on.
2. Be sure the printer is on line.
3. Check cables at the printer and the computer. Sometimes a loose cable will indicate the presence of the printer but will not print.
4. Check for out of ribbon or out of paper if your printer has these shutdown features.
5. Some printers may be waiting for fonts to download. Usually there is an indicator light on the printer that flashes. This indicates some activity is occurring.

If WORD acts as if it has printed but shows the message "0 lines and 0 words" or "1 line and 0 words," check the following:

1. Select the Print Option command. Check the "range" field. If it is set for Selections and nothing in your document has been highlighted, nothing will be printed. If you want to print a selection, return to the document and highlight the area you wish to print.
2. Select the Print Option command. Check the range field. If it is set for "Pages," the page

number field must have a page number or range that actually exists in the document.

3. If you are doing a Print Merge, check to see that there is data in the data document. Load the data document, using the Transfer Load command.

4. If you are using a laser printer and are in landscape mode, check the page length and width with the Format Division Margin command. The length should be set to 8.5 inches and the width should be 11 inches.

5. Check to be sure the whole document has not been created as a running head. This does not happen very often, but may be a possibility. This will be indicated with a caret, "^", symbol in the left hand margin of every paragraph. If this is the case, press Shift + F10 to highlight the whole document. Select the Format Running-head command. Change the "position" field to None. If you did require a running head in the document, return to the specific line and reformat it with the Format Running-head command.

Is there a quick way to preview my print out?

In WORD 5.0 there is a new feature for previewing your document before printing. It provides a full page or optionally a two page on-screen display of the document. The text may be difficult to read due to size, but it is a good way to see the page layout with relative print positions and graphics displayed. In addition, you can see many things not shown in the normal display, including the relative margins, running heads, footnotes, page numbers, line numbers, side-by-side paragraphs, multiple text columns, graphics, borders, revision marks, paragraph, and character formatting.

The preview mode, however, does not have any zoom feature so most smaller type fonts are unreadable in the preView mode. Microsoft has indicated this may be added in a future revision.

To display your document in the preview mode and view two pages at a time:

1. Select the Print preView command.
2. Press PageDown to view additional pages and PageUp to view prior pages.
3. Choose Exit when your preview is complete.

To view just one page at a time:

1. Select the Print preView command.
2. Choose Options.
3. Select 1-page in the "display" field.
4. Press Enter.

How can I print a document and continue editing another one?

WORD has a feature to permit printing while you are editing. It is the "queued" field in the Print Options menu. Both the editing and printing process are slowed down while using this feature.

WORD creates a temporary print file on the document disk. The number of files you can queue is related to the available disk space. A message is displayed if you run out of space.

To queue documents:
1. Select the Print Option command.
2. Change the "queued" field to Yes.

To turn off the Queueing:
1. Select the Print Option command.
2. Change the "queued" field to No.

You may pause printing with Print Queue Pause command or stop the printout entirely with Print Queue Stop command. To restart after a pause, select the Print Queue Restart command.

My printer keeps printing summary sheets. What commands do I use to eliminate the summary sheet from being printed?

WORD's summary sheet provides information which permits you to find a document easily, using the Library Document-retrieval feature. The summary sheet may be turned off at two levels. You may stop it from printing and you may stop the summary sheet from displaying when you save a document.

To turn off the printing of the summary sheet:

1. Select the Print Options command.
2. Choose No in the "summary sheet" field.

To turn off the display of the summary sheet when you save documents:

1. Select the Options command.
2. Choose No in the "summary sheet" field.

Summary sheets are very helpful if you have quite a few files to manage. With the Library Document-retrieval command, you can search for documents based on author, operator, key words, creation date, document text, and revision date.

I would like to print labels on my laser printer. The laser printer label stock comes three labels in a row. How do I get Word to print three across?

Mailing lists are prepared using a data document and a main document. The main document contains the printing instructions and the data document contains the addresses. To format the main document for a 1 inch label on an 8.5 x 11 inch sheet:

1. Select the Format Division Margin command.

2. Set the "top" field to 1 inch the "left" to .5 inch, the "right" to 0 and the "bottom" to 0.

3. Enter the Data statement and the first label record as follows:

```
<<DATA ADDRESS.DOC>><<name>>
<<address>>
<<city>>,<<ST>><<ZIP>>
```

The ADDRESS.DOC is the name of the data file. The "name," "address," etc. are the field names of the data in the data file.

4. Enter three blank lines and repeat the field date again as follows:

```
<<NEXT>><<name>>
```

```
<<address>>
<<city>>, <<ST>><<ZIP>>
```

The NEXT command is important because it tells WORD to select the next data record.

5.   Enter three more blank lines. Highlight this last entry from the NEXT command through the three blank lines.

6.   Select the Copy command. Move the cursor just below the last entry.

7.   Press Insert seven times to duplicate the field entry. The left column has now been produced.

8.   Select the Format Division Layout command.

9.   Set the "number of columns" field to 3, "space between columns" to 0, and "division break" to column.

10. Press Insert nine times in each new column to insert the field data for every location a label is to be printed. This produces the second and third columns.

11. Select Transfer save to save the main document.

12. Select Print Merge Print, to merge the data.

Note: Since many laser printers have different starting points, you may have to play with the top margin value. You also may be able to format one or two more labels per column.

Chapter 11

Style Sheets

Style Sheets, Applications and Definition

What are Style Sheets used for?

Style sheets may be used for storing commonly used formats for different types of letters, memos, documentation, forms, and newsletters.

Style Sheets are used by WORD to store information about the specific format used in a document. For example, if you normally use a 1 inch margin for your documents, but for a specific type of letter, 1.5 inches is required, a style sheet can be used to save this format. For just one change to the document format, the style sheet may not be worth the trouble. However, if you have extensive character, paragraph and division format changes, the style sheet is absolutely essential.

The style sheet that is available when you execute WORD is called the NORMAL.STY style sheet. It provides the default settings when WORD is executed. These settings also may be changed if you regularly use a specific format.

Style sheets are created, modified, and saved in the Gallery window. This window is accessed with Gallery command. Each newly created style sheet is saved with a different style sheet name.

With each style sheet is a series of codes which correspond to a specific format. The codes may be viewed in the Gallery window. They are located on the left hand side of the screen. Formats are categorized by character, paragraph, and division. To execute the desired format, the Alt key is held down and the two letters corresponding to the desired code are typed.

I loaded a new style sheet but nothing happened
in the document. How do I get the style sheet
to activate?

Style sheets may be attached to a document
in one of two ways. The easiest way is to:

1. Select the Format Stylesheet Attach
command.
2. Press F1 to see the list of available style
sheets.
3. Choose the desired sheet. Press Enter.

To apply the various styles:

1. Highlight the text you wish to format.
2. Select the Format Stylesheet command.
3. Choose the Character, Paragraph, or
Division option.
4. Press F1 to choose the appropriate variant
option. Select the option and press Enter.

You also may attach a style sheet in the
following manner:

1. Select the Gallery command.
2. Select the Transfer Load command.
3. Press F1 to see the list.
4. Make your selection and press Enter.
5. Select the Exit command to leave the
Gallery window.

6. Type Y in response to the question to attach the style sheet.

To attach the styles displayed in the Gallery window:

1. Highlight the text to be formatted.
2. Hold down the Alt key and type the two letter code associated with the desired format.

Our sales department uses two different formats for its letters. How do we use a style sheet to maintain the two options?

Create a separate style sheet for each letter. Creating a new style sheet for each letter format is much like formatting the original document. Once completed, the document formatting process is distinctly accelerated.

Here is the basic way to create a new style sheet using the Gallery menu:

1. Select the Gallery command.

2. If a style sheet is present, remove it with the Transfer Clear command.

3. To add a format, select the Insert command.

4. Enter the one or two letter key code you will use to execute the format.

5. Select the option of Character, Paragraph, or Division to be formatted. Change the format as you would in a document.

6. Skip the variant assignment.

7. Enter a remark in the "remark" field to remind you of what the format command does.

8. Press Enter when the format is completed.

9. Repeat steps 3-8 for each additional format.

10. To save the style sheet, select the Transfer Save command and type the new name.

11. Select the Exit command to leave the Gallery window.

When I start a new WORD session, I would like to have margins and a printer font different from those provided by WORD. How can these be changed?

Every time WORD is executed it automatically uses the style sheet called NORMAL.STY. This style sheet contains a preset group of formats for every new document. By loading another style sheet, other options may be used. You also can change the NORMAL.STY sheet with the following:

1. Select the Gallery command.
2. If you have been using another style sheet, load the NORMAL.STY style sheet using the Transfer Load command in the Gallery menu.
3. Select the Insert command.
4. Go to the "usage" field and select your choice of the Character, Paragraph, or Division to change. If you are changing the margins, select Division. If you are changing the character fonts, select paragraph. (In this case the Standard Paragraph contains the character format.)
5. Go to the variant field and press F1 to see a list of choices.
6. Select the "Standard" option or other variant you wish to change. Press Enter.

7.   Select the Format Character and Format Division commands and change the desired options for each part of the style sheet. Press Enter.

8.   Select the Transfer Save command to save the changes.

9.   Select the Exit command to leave the Gallery window.

I have written a letter with a different layout than I normally use as a standard. Is there any way to record this format for future use without having to start over with a new style sheet?

WORD has the ability to capture the formatting for a document you have created by entering the keystrokes automatically to the style sheet. To do this:

1. Highlight the text from which you wish to capture the format.
2. Select the Format Stylesheet Record command.
3. Enter a one or two character code in the "key code" field. You will use this code later to recall the format information.
4. Move to the "usage" field and select Character, Paragraph, or Division formatting.
5. If you wish to select a different variant than WORD proposes, move to the "variant" field and either type a different number or press F1 and select from the list.
6. Move to the "remark" field and enter a note indicating the format purpose.
7. Press Enter to create the style.
Note: If all of the character formats are the same in a specific paragraph, the paragraph format may contain the character format options.

Is there a way I can check what style has been applied to each part of the document?

To see what format has been applied to specific parts of the document, you must turn on the Style Bar:

1. Select the Options command.
2. Move to the "show style bar" field and select Yes.
3. Press Enter.

The style bar shows the selected styles on the left hand side of the screen. The styles are represented using the same code as they are stored in the style sheet. For example, a division code would show by the division marker and a paragraph format shows next to the appropriate paragraph.

To view the codes, select the Gallery command. Then select Exit to leave the Gallery window.

To turn off the Style bar:

1. Select the Options command.
2. Move to the "show style bar" field and select No.
3. Press Enter.

Chapter 12

Tables and Indexes

Tables and Indexes, Applications and Definition

What are table and index features of WORD used for?

The manual process of indexing a document can be very time consuming. By marking each phrase or key word you wish to place in an index, WORD can compile the index for you. The real value of this feature is discovered when modifications to the document change all the index values. All that you have to do is recompile the index.

The table feature works similarly to the index feature. By using different marking codes, you can build multiple tables. One may be the Table of Contents, another a table of diagrams of photos and yet another a table of formulas.

Both tables and indexes are built by first marking each entry in the document with a special code. This code is then formatted as hidden text. Once all the entries have been identified, a table or index is created, using either the Library Table or Library Index command.

Our plant operating procedure manual frequently changes due to new product lines and new systems. Modifications to the manual affects the page numbering of the Table of Contents. What steps do I take in WORD to prevent having to renumber constantly?

The Table of Contents feature of WORD permits you to automatically build a table from your document. This means you also can recompile the table whenever changes are made to the document.

To create the table, you must indicate the phrases or section headings in your document that you would like to include in the Table. (You also may use your outline if one is available.) The table entry is indicated with the code ".C.". This code then is formatted as hidden text. To indicate the end of the text to appear in the table, a semicolon, paragraph mark, or division mark is used. If one is not present, then a semicolon must be added as hidden text.

Once all the phrases are indicated, the table is compiled with the Library Table command. The resulting table will appear at the end of your document.

To create a table entry:

1. Move to the first letter of the phrase to be included in the table.

2. Press Alt + E (or Alt + XE) to format the code as hidden text.

3. Type .C.

4. Press Alt + Spacebar to turn off the hidden formatting.

5. Move to the end of the phrase. Type a semicolon unless the end of the phrase is an endmark already.

To compile the table:

1. Select the Library Table command.

2. Choose the Codes option in the "from" field.

3. Choose Yes in the "page numbers" field.

4. Press Enter to begin the compilation of the table. The table appears at the end of the document.

Note: Indexes are created virtually the same way except that ".C." is replaced with ".I." and the Library Table command is replaced with the Library Index command.

I'm trying to create an index with sub entries to specific topics. How is this done?

To create an index category, create the index entry with the category name included with hidden index code. To separate different levels, a colon is used. For example, if you wish to sort information about the subject Maps in a separate category, Maps is a category identified in the hidden text portion of the index code. If the indexed word is "topical," the following example shows how to format the entry:

There is a new interest in .i.Maps:topical; maps. The ".i.Maps" is formatted as hidden text as is the semicolon at the end of topical.

You may have as many subentries as you require. Each level must be separated with another colon.

Note: If there is no single main entry and the main entry is associated only with a lower level entry, no page number shows for the main entry. Map with a sublevel always attached to it will not show a page number.

There seems to be a tremendous number of keystrokes involved in the index procedure. Are there any shortcuts?

WORD provides two macros for creating tables and indexes. They are available in the MACRO.GLY glossary. To load MACRO.GLY:

1. Select the Transfer Glossary Load command.
2. Press F1 and select MACRO.GLY.
3. Press Enter.

The macro supplied for creating table entries is called "toc_entry.mac." To use the macro:

1. Highlight the phrase for the table entry.
2. Press Control + TE to execute the macro.

The macro supplied for creating table entries is called "index_entry.mac." To use the macro:

1. Highlight the phrase for the index entry.
2. Press Control + IE to execute the macro.

Note: It is a good idea to save the document before designating text as index or table entries.

I am writing support manuals. The manual is written as one document per chapter. How can I apply Tables or Indexes to them?

While it definitely is easier to get around smaller documents, automated tables and indexes don't lend themselves well to multiple file documents. When creating each chapter, proceed to enter the table and index codes to the appropriate text. When the document is finished, you must merge all the individual files into one document. To do this:

1. Select Transfer Load to load the first document.

2. Press Control + PageDown to go to the end of the document.

3. Select the Transfer Merge command and enter the name of the next document to load.

4. Repeat steps 2 and 3 until all the files are loaded.

Once all the files are loaded, you may proceed to create the table with the Library Table command and the index with the Library Index command. Then you will have to move the Table to the front of the document.

Since much of the organizational work for a document is done in the outline process, is it practical to use the outline as the Table of Contents?

If you have created an outline along with your document, it may be converted into the Table of Contents. The outline is a quick and ideal way not only to keep up the organizational maintenance of the document, but it is the fastest way to build your Table of Contents.

Before converting the outline to a table, you first should review it to insure that all the headings you want to have are included. Eliminate any unwanted headings.

To compile the Table of Contents off the outline:

1. Select the Library Table command.
2. Change the "from" field to Outline.
3. Press Enter.

Each level in the outline will be appropriately indented in the table. The resulting table may be copied to the beginning of the document.

Chapter 13

Windows

Windows, Applications

For what types of situations would windows be useful?

Windows give WORD an added dimension to word processing. You can have multiple documents available on or off screen for reference, for moving information back and forth, or simply to work on them at the same time without having to save and reload.

Up to eight windows may be open at the same time. Each window may divide the screen horizontally or vertically.

You can use windows to:

- Create memos or notes to yourself.
- View a main document and merge document at the same time to check field names.

- Copy text from one document to another.
- Work on two parts of a document at the same time.
- Display one document while annotating it in another window.
- View footnotes at the same time as you work in the document.
- Display an outline and its document at the same time.
- Display a document with and without hidden text.

When our weekly reports contain repetitive information, how can I use windows to place the old information in the new document?

Copying data from one document to another is one of the outstanding benefits of windows. To accomplish this, you must create a second window. The document to be copied from is loaded in the second window. Follow this procedure to copy from one document to another:

1. Load the document you wish to copy to, using the Transfer Load command.

2. Select the Window Split Horizontal command.

3. In the "at line" field, enter the number 20 if you are working on a 43 line screen and 12 if you are working with a 25 line screen.

4. In the "clear new window," select the Yes option.

5. Load the document you wish to copy from into this window.

6. Highlight the text you wish to copy.

7. Select the Copy command and press Enter.

8. Press F1 to move to window number 1.

9. Place the cursor where you wish to enter the text.

10. Press the Insert key.

11. To close the window, select the Window Close command.

12. Type 2 in the "window number" field. Press Enter.

I currently use a mouse with Word. Is there a way to use the mouse to create and move around windows?

To create a window with a mouse, place the arrow on the right or top border. (Rulers must be turned off for the top border mouse to appear.) The arrow turns into a box and the window can be created by clicking either button.

Placing the arrow at the top border creates vertical windows at the pointer location. Placing the arrow on the right border creates a horizontal window at the pointer location.

To open another window for the same document, press the left button. To open an empty window, press the right button.

To close a window with the mouse, position the mouse on the top or right border and press both buttons.

To move a window with the mouse:

1. Point to the bottom right corner of the window where the arrow turns into two crossed double arrows.

2. Hold down either button.

3. Move the pointer to the new location and release the button.

Sometimes after I have created a window, it appears too small to use. Can I make it larger without closing and reopening it?

To change a window size with a mouse, you point to the bottom right hand corner of the window and hold down either button. "Drag" the pointer to the new window corner location and release.

To change the size of a window manually:

1. Select the Window Move command.

2. Type the window number in the field labelled "lower right corner of window #".

3. Move to the "to row" field to move a horizontal border and to the "to column" field to move a vertical border.

4. Press F1 to make a highlight appear in the window border.

5. Use the cursor (direction) keys to move the border to the desired location.

6. Press Enter.

Note: You also may enter a row or column number in the "to row" or "to column" field instead of using the cursor keys.

You also can use the Zoom, Control + F1 to see more of the screen.

Windows, Zoom

I have several windows displayed. One of the smaller ones is difficult to read. How can I see more of a window?

Zooming on a window brings the window to full screen, hiding all the other open windows. Before zooming on a window, first it must be selected. To select a window, press F1 repeatedly until the desired window is displayed.

To zoom on the selected window, press Control + F1.

To return to the open windows display, press Control + F1 again.

A zoomed window also may be toggled with all the other open windows. Each time the F1 key is pressed, the next sequential window is displayed full screen.

Index

Additions 13
Address Envelopes 125
Alignment 70
All Save 12
Alt x
Apply Styles 139
ASCII 15,43,53
ASCII Character File 53
ASCII File, Editing 43
ASCII Mailing Lists 105
Ask 106
Autoexec 1,2
Autoexec.bat 2
Automatic Execution 1-2
Automatic File Load 3
Automatic Page Break 3
Automatic Spelling
    Correction 21
Autosave 45
Back to Back Printing 119
Back-up Files 46
Backspace Key 23
Backspace Not Working 23
BAK Files 46
BAK Files 51
Batch Files 2
Beginning WORD 1-12
Beginning WORD,
    Automatic Execution
    1-2
Beginning WORD,
    Automatic File Load 3
Beginning WORD,
    Automatic Page
    Breaks 4

Beginning WORD, Cursor
    Speed 5
Beginning WORD, Display
    Characteristics 6-7
Beginning WORD, End
    Mark 8
Beginning WORD,
    Measurement 9
Beginning WORD, Mouse
    Speed 10
Beginning WORD, Printer
    Display 11
Beginning WORD,
    Transfer 12
Blank Line 127
Blank Pages 107
Blank Set of Data 107
Block Letters 81
Bold Text x
Borders 6,55
Boxes 55,88
Bullet_list.mac macro 121
Bullets 121
Caps Lock 25
Captions 83
Capture 84,91
CAPTURE.COM 84,91
Case Changes 25
Case Sensitivity 36
Change Default Directory
    12
character_test.mac 29
Chevrons 104
Color 6
Columns 26,57
Columns, Moving

26
Columns, Multiple 57
Command Field Editing 28
Commands   ix
Control Codes 129
Control+Shift+Enter 4
Copying Using Windows 157
Create Style Sheets 141
Create, Tables and Indexes 149
Creating Glossaries 95
Cursor Speed 5
Data Directory 47
Data Document 103
DATA instruction 103
DATA Statement 108
DATE 123
Date Stamps 123
DATEPRINT 123
Default 58
Default Directory 12,47
Default Tab 9,60
Default Type Fonts 58
Default, Style Sheet 142
Delete, Files 12
Delete, Macros and Glossaries 96
Diamond Symbol 8
Dictionary 13-22
Dictionary, Additions 13-14
Dictionary, ASCII 15-16
Dictionary, Document 13
Dictionary, Foreign Language 17
Dictionary, Location 18
Dictionary, Main 13
Dictionary, Partial Checks 19

Dictionary, Proper Names 20
Dictionary, Remember 21
Dictionary, Special User 13
Dictionary, Synonyms 22
Dictionary, Thesaurus 22
Dictionary, User 13-14
Directory 47,48
Directory, Creating 49
Directory, Management 49
Disabled Mouse 10
Disk Full 51
Display Characteristics 6
Division 8
Document Dictionary 20
Document Disk Full 51
Document Retrieval 49,134
Draft Mode   124
Drawing LInes 61
Dual Floppies 52
Edit 97
Edit, Backspace Not Working 23-24
Edit, Caps Lock 25
Edit, Columns 26-27
Edit, Command Fields 28
Edit, Extended Character Set 29
Edit, Hidden Text 30
Edit, Highlighting Text 31
Edit, Macros and Glossaries 97
Edit, Mouse Edit 32
Edit, Multiple Documents 33-34
Edit, Paragraph Marker 35
Edit, Search and Replace Not Working 36
Edit, Search for Formats 37-38

Edit, Undo 41
Edit, Vertical Lines 39-40
Edit, Word Count 42
Editing 23-42
End Mark 8
End of Document 8
Endnotes 66
Envelopes 125
Errors, Merging 108
Esc ix
Extended Character Set
    29,121
Extending the Highlight 31
Extra Blank Line 127
Fields x
File, ASCII   43-44
File, Autosave 45
File, BAK Files 46
File, Default Directory 47
File, Directory 48
File, Directory
    Management 49-50
File, Disk Full 51
File, Extensions 17
File, Laptops 52
File, Load 3
File, Management 49
File, Modem 53
File, TMP Files 54
Files   43-54
Finding Solutions viii
Font Selections 64
Fonts, Default 58
Fonts, Not Printing 63
Fonts, Page Numbers 73
Footnotes 66
Foreign Language 17
Format 55-80
Format Border Box
    55,88,90

Format Character 64,98
Format Division 8
Format Division Layout
    57,73
Format Division Margins 4
Format Division Page-
    number 73
Format pOsition 76,86
Format RepLace 37
Format Tabs Set 39
Format, Boxes 55-56
Format, Columns 57
Format, Default Tabs 60
Format, Defaults 58-59
Format, Drawing Lines 61-
    62
Format, Font Selections 64-
    65
Format, Fonts Not Printing
    63
Format, Footnotes 66
Format, Hanging Indent 67
Format, Hidden Text 68
Format, Justify Lists 69
Format, Margin Change 70
Format, Numbering 71-72
Format, Page Numbers 73-
    74
Format, Preprinted Forms
    75-76
Format, Running Heads
    77-78
Format, Speed Format
    Keys 79
Format, Tab Set 80
Formats 137
Formatting 79,129
Forms 75
Frames 86
Gallery Command 138

163

Glossary 93
Glossary, Create 95
Graphic Import 87
Graphics 81-92
Graphics Characters 29
Graphics Mode 5,10
Graphics, Block Letters 81-82
Graphics, Captions 83
Graphics, Capture 84-85
Graphics, Frames 86
Graphics, Graphic Import 87
Graphics, Line Drawing 88
Graphics, Printing 89
Graphics, Shading 90
Graphics, Sizing 91
Graphics, Vertical Lines 92
Hanging Indent 67
Hidden Text 30,68,75,128
Hidden Text, Formatting 30
Highlighting Text 30,31
How to Use This Book viii-x
IF Command 111
Import Screens 84
INCLUDE Command 111
Index Macro 152
Index, Subentries 151
Indexes 147-154
Indexes, Indented Entries 151
Indexes, Multiple Documents 153
Insert Mode 24
Italic Text 37
Justify Lists 69
Labels 109,135
Labels, Three Up 135

Landscape Orientation 125
Laptops 52
Large Block Letter 81
Laser Printer 63,89,70,125,136,135
Layout Mode 11
Leading Tab Characters 61
Library Link Graphic 85,89
Library Spell 14
Library thEsaurus 22
Line Drawing 61,88
Lines 61,92
Load 3,12
Location of Dictionary 18
Lost Document 54
Lotus Graphs 87
LY 68
Macro 64,93
MACRO.GLY 29,152
MACROS & GLOSSARIES, Applications and Definition 93-94
MACROS & GLOSSARIES, Creating Glossaries 95
MACROS & GLOSSARIES, Delete 96
MACROS & GLOSSARIES, Edit 97
MACROS & GLOSSARIES, Format Characters 98
MACROS & GLOSSARIES, Merge 99
MACROS & GLOSSARIES, Naming 100

MACROS & GLOSSARIES, Saving 101-102
Macros and Glossaries 93-102
Mail Merge 104
Mailing Labels 109
Main Dictionary 13
Main Document 103
Manual Page Break 4
Margin Change 70
Margin Settings 58
Margins, Default 58
Measurement 9
Menu ix, 6
Menu Command ix
Merge 12,33,99
Merge Field 106
Merge, Macros and Glossaries 99
Merge, Selective 111
Merging 103-112
Merging Documents 33
Merging, Applications and Definition 103-104
Merging, ASCII Mailing Lists 105
Merging, Ask 106
Merging, Blank Pages 107
Merging, Errors 108
Merging, Include 111-112
Merging, Labels 109-110
Modem 53
Mouse 10,31,158
Mouse Speed 10
Mouse, Disabled 10
Mouse, Edit 32
Mouse, Highlighting 31
Multiple Columns 57
Multiple Documents 33

Naming 100
Naming, Macros and Glossaries 100
Near Letter Quality 124
NEXT Command 136
Non-printing Symbols 26
NORMAL.GLY 3,99,198
NORMAL.STY 58,142
Nothing Prints 130
Numbering 71
Options Menu 6
Organization viii
OT Mode 23
Outline 113-118,154
Outline, Applications 113
Outline, Body Text 115
Outline, Document Text 114-115
Outline, Levels and Numbering 116
Outline, Outlining Existing Documents 117-118
Outline, View Model 117
Overtype Mode 23
Page Breaks 4
Page Number Fonts 73
Page Numbers 73
Paragraph Format 35
Paragraph Marker 35,98
Paragraph, Hanging 67
Path Names 48
Pitch 9
PRD File 52,63,129
Preprinted Forms 75
Preview Print Out 132
Print Hidden Text 30
Print PreView 11
Print View 132
Print While Editing 133
Printer 119-136

Printer, Back to Back
    Printing 119-120
Printer, Bullets 121
Printer, Changes 122
Printer, Date Stamps 123
Printer, Display 11
Printer, Draft Mode 124
Printer, Envelopes 125-126
Printer, Extra Blank Line
    127
Printer, Format 122
Printer, Hidden Text 128
Printer, Imbedded Control
    Codes 129
Printer, Nothing Prints
    130-131
Printer, Print View 132
Printer, Queueing 133
Printer, Summary Sheets
    134
Printer, Three Up Labels
    135-136
Proper Names 20
Queueing 133
Quick Key ix
Record Style Sheet 144
Recovery Process 45
Remember Misspellings 21
Rename Files 12
Repagination 4
Replace Paragraph Marks
    44
Retrieval of Information
    33-34
Revision Marks 15
Running Head, Disappears
    78
Running Head, Doesn't
    Print 77
Running Heads 73,77,78

Save 12,45
Save, Macros and
    Glossaries 101
Save, Misspelled Words 21
Scrap 26
Scratch files 54
Search and Replace Not
    Working 36
Search for Formats 37
Selective Merging 111
Selective Spell Checks 19
Shade a Box 90
Shift+Enter 55,69
Show Layout 11,68
Show Non-printing
    Symbols 35
Show Ruler 80
Single Character
    Formatting 79
Size Graphics 91
Size Windows 159
Slow Mouse 10
Soft Carriage Return 55,69
Solutions viii
Special Graphics
    Characters 29
Speed Format x,79,80
Spell Check 13-21
Spell Check, Partial 19
SPELL-AM.LEX 18
Split Window 33
Spread Sheets 15
Style Bar 145
Style Sheets x,137-146
Style Sheets, Applications/
    Definition 137-138
Style Sheets, Apply 139-
    140
Style Sheets, Create 141
Style Sheets, Defaults 142-

143
Style Sheets, Record 144
Style Sheets, Style Bar 145-146
Sub-directories 48
Sublevels of an Outline 116
Summary Sheet 50,134
Syntax ix
Tab Measurement 9
Tab Set 80
Table Macro 152
Table of Contents, Outline 154
TABLES & INDEXES, Applications and Definition 147-148
TABLES & INDEXES, Create 149-150
TABLES & INDEXES, Indented Entries 151
TABLES & INDEXES, Macro 152
TABLES & INDEXES, Multiple Documents 153
TABLES & INDEXES, Outline 154
Tables and Indexes 147-154
Tabs 9
Tabs, Default 60
Text Display 6
Text Mode 10
Text Only 53
Text Runoff 11
Thesaurus 22,52
TMP Files 51,54
Transfer 12
Transfer All Save 12
Transfer Command 12
Transfer Glossary Save 101
Transfer Merge 33,66
Transfer Save 45
TYPE Command 17
Type Fonts 63
Type Styles 9
Underlining 37,62
Undo 35,41
User Dictionary 13-14,18,20
Vertical Lines 39,92
View Paragraph Markers 35
Windows 12,114,155-160
Windows, Applications 155-156
Windows, Copying 157
Windows, Mouse 158
Windows, Size 159
Windows, Split 33
Windows, Zoom 160
WORD 4.0 127
WORD 4.0 8,25,70
Word Count 42
Word Count Macro 42
WORD Spell Check 15
Zoom 160